FOOTBALL ENGLISH

Soccer Vocabulary for Learners of English

Tom Challenger

ISBN 978-3-9503382-0-1

Eniko Books
Tom Challenger
Diehlgasse 30/10, 1050, Wien, Austria

To contact the author please visit: footballenglish.org

First published 2012

Cover photo by Model Photo: Colourbox.com

Illustrations by the author

CONTENTS

HOW TO USE THIS BOOK

This book is a collection of vocabulary exercises. The exercises are designed to practise the English for football you already know, or introduce you to new football terms in a memorable, realistic context. They are carefully designed so you can use the contexts (sentences, match reports, pictures etc.), logic and your knowledge of football to maximise your learning.

You can do the chapters in any order you wish. It is suggested that you start with the topics which are most relevant to your needs or interests.

The solutions (answers) to each exercise are at the end of the book. Try your best to do the whole exercise before you look at the answers! This will maximise the learning experience because the more you look at the contexts and use logic to find the answers, the deeper the learning will be. Think of each exercise like a puzzle.

Each chapter has a difficulty level: 1, 2 or 3. The easier exercises contain the most useful English for football vocabulary, the harder exercises contain football vocabulary which isn't so necessary for basic communication but is used a lot by advanced speakers and in newspaper articles etc. If you have an intermediate level of English reading skills (i.e. about B1) then you can do all of the levels. The more difficult levels will take you longer and you may need to use a dictionary to help you sometimes.

If you find the easier exercises very easy, then they are still worth doing because then you can concentrate on getting the phrases exactly correct, e.g. noticing that we say attack**ing** midfielder and not *attack midfielder; a **well**-deserved victory, not *a good-deserved victory; he **got** the equaliser not *he made the equaliser, etc.

In this book players are referred to by their surnames, e.g. "**Smith** scored", "**Williams** was a substitute". Teams are referred to using the common team name endings: United, Rovers, City, Wanderers, Albion and Athletic, e.g. "**Wanderers** are in good form at the moment", "**Albion** have signed two new players".

Please contact me at *footballenglish.org* if you have any comments or questions, where you can also find helpful English for football learning resources. And if you would like to recommend the book to other people then please leave a review on the website where you bought the book (e.g. amazon.de, amazon.es etc.).

I hope you enjoy using this book to improve your Football English!

Tom Challenger, 2012.

Difficulty Levels

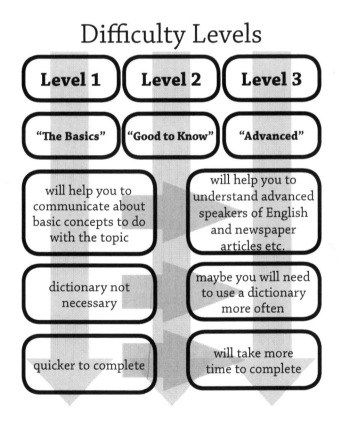

Level 1	Level 2	Level 3
"The Basics"	"Good to Know"	"Advanced"
will help you to communicate about basic concepts to do with the topic		will help you to understand advanced speakers of English and newspaper articles etc.
dictionary not necessary		maybe you will need to use a dictionary more often
quicker to complete		will take more time to complete

For Kati & Eni

1. Kicking & Moving The Ball

Difficulty level 1: "The Basics"
Ex. 1 Match the words and phrases with their definitions:

1. To shoot B
2. To pass back
3. To cross
4. To pass
5. To touch the ball
6. To volley the ball
7. To hit the ball
8. To half-volley the ball
9. To hit the ball long
10. To chest the ball

a half-volley

A. To make contact with the ball, e.g. kick it or head it.
B. To kick the ball in order to score.
C. To kick the ball while it is in the air.
D. To kick the ball into the centre so someone on your team can try to score a goal.
E. To kick the ball to a player on your team.
F. To kick the ball immediately after it has bounced.
G. To control the ball with your upper-body.
H. To pass the ball a great distance in a forward or diagonal direction.
I. To kick the ball, usually to kick it hard.
J. To kick the ball to your goalkeeper.

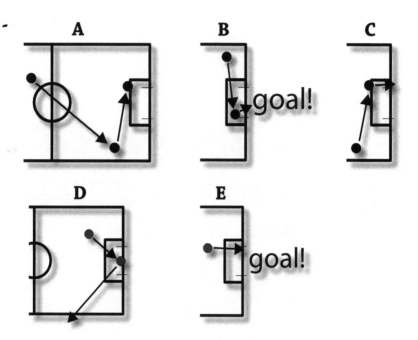

Ex. 2 Match the sentences below to the pictures, and fill in the gaps (the answers to *Ex.1* will help you):

1. Smith passed it _back_ to his goalkeeper who hit the ball out for a throw-in. *picture D*
2. Adams c_____ the ball from the left, finding Robins who headed in from close range.
3. He had time to take a t_____ before hitting it firmly into the bottom left corner.
4. He met Smith's cross with a half-v_____ which went just wide.
5. Robins got on the end of Smith's l_____-ball and crossed for Adams.

Ex. 3 This is part of a half-time television analysis. Find the words & phrases that are described below (the picture is a diagram of the action being described):

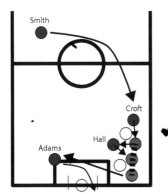

"...Smith's high, diagonal ball **upfield** found Croft sprinting down the left, who cleverly flicked the ball past his marker on to Robins and played a quick one-two with Hall. A perfect first-touch and an explosive burst of pace took Robins clear of the helpless Richards who could do nothing to stop a low, hard cross reaching Adams on the edge of the area. Adams surprised the keeper with a well-placed, first-time chip into the top-left corner..."

1. [An adjective] in a forward direction... : _upfield_
2. [A verb] to touch the ball very lightly in order to pass it to another player (using the power already on the ball)... : _CROSSED_
3. [Two-word noun] a move where player A passes to player B, who quickly passes the ball back to player A again... : _one-Two_
4. [Two-word noun] the first 'kick' to bring the ball under control... : _First touch_
5. [Adjective+noun] kicking the ball into the centre, near the goal, along the ground... : _Low CROSS_
6. [Adjective] without taking a first touch... : _____
7. [Noun] a shot which is kicked delicately over the goalkeeper... : _chip_

Ex. 4 These are sentences from match reports. Match the words & phrases **in bold** with their definitions below:
(Example 6=A)

...his third goal followed shortly afterwards as he sprinted on to Allen's [1]**lofted pass** out of defence, turned and [2]**fire**d a right-footed drive into the bottom corner...

...Some slick play from Athletic culminated in Hill [3]**slipping the ball through** to Perry, who blasted it high over the United goal from the edge of the area...

...Henderson put Mason through on goal with a delightful [4]**slide-rule pass** but his left-footed shot was easily saved by Armstrong...

...Lamberton earned the visitors all three points with a very late goal, guiding in Daniels' [5]**teasing** cross with only two minutes left on the clock...

...Lamberton had been on the field only three minutes when he played [6]**a perfectly weighted pass** to Bowen, who finished confidently...

...This was impressive play from Wanderers who were [7]**knocking the ball around** nicely and causing Rovers problems...

...Hall tried to [8]**curl** the free kick into the top-left corner, but there wasn't enough bend on it to beat the keeper...

6 A. A pass which is not too hard, but not too soft.

1 B. A long, high pass.

7 C. Keeping the ball for a long period by passing the ball skilfully to each other.

3 D. Passing the ball very skilfully, but quite slowly, along the ground through a small space between the defenders.

4 E. A very skilful pass along the ground which goes through a small space between defenders.

5 F. Describes a dangerous, quite slow ball in the air towards the opponent's goal which is difficult for the defenders or goalkeeper to reach.

8 G. To kick the ball so it doesn't go in a straight line, but curves in the air.

2 H. To shoot or pass very powerfully.

Ex. 5 Use the explanations of the words & phrases to fill the gaps in the sentences from match reports(use each word/phrase only once):

A reverse pass: The player doesn't pass the ball in the direction that he is running in, but passes it suddenly about 90° to the left or to the right.

To dink [the ball]: The ball is kicked very lightly and delicately.

A punt: A forceful, inaccurate, long kick.

[To pass down] the inside-right channel: The pass is quite deep in the opponent's half and between where the left centre-back and left-back (on the other team) normally are.

A knock-on: A player touches the ball lightly to change its direction by a small amount. He hopes the ball will go to another player on his team.

To ping [the ball]: To pass the ball forcefully and accurately, often over a large distance.

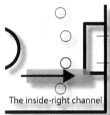

1. Rovers are _pinging_ it around midfield nicely now and Wanderers just can't get hold of the ball.
2. Evans dinked the ball over the keeper but there wasn't quite enough power to take it across the line before Shepard intercepted.
3. McDowell changed the direction of play by finding Jarvis, who had made a diagonal run, with a clever reverse pass
4. City are having no luck with their tactic of trying speculative punts up to the front two.
5. United scored from their first corner of the game when Small's _____ at the near post was bundled in by Jennings.
6. Carver found some space in the box when getting on the end of a perfectly weighted pass down _____ but could only shoot wide.

2. Positions

Ex 1. Match the names of positions to the correct place on the diagram:

1. forward J&K
2. right-back E
3. centre-midfield G M
4. goalkeeper A
5. left-midfield f
6. centre-back C D
7. left-back B
8. right-midfield I

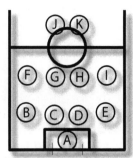

Ex. 2 Match these position names to their descriptions:

1. goalie C
2. sweeper / libero H
3. full-back K
4. centre-half D
5. holding midfielder / midfield anchor f
6. second striker / "the number 10" I
7. winger E
8. centre-forward A
9. a target man J
10. attacking midfielder G
11. wing-back B

A. A striker (who plays the furthest forward).
B. A left or right-back who should also attack.
C. The goalkeeper.
D. Another word for centre-back.
E. A midfielder who plays wide on the right/left and should provide lots of crosses for the striker/s.
F. A midfielder with a defensive role.
G. A midfielder with an offensive role.
H. A defender who plays behind the other defenders.
I. A forward who plays just behind the other striker, but in front of the midfield.
J. A striker (normally tall) whose role is to receive long balls from the defence.
K. Another word for a right/left-back.

3. Describing a Game

Difficulty level 1: "The Basics"

Ex. 1 These are some things fans say just after watching their team play. Match each sentence with the descriptions:

1. "That was a great **comeback**!" E
2. "I think the **scoreline** was unfair." [It was 0-2 to the other team]
3. "The **pace** of the game was too **high** for us."
4. "We **dominate**d the first half."
5. "That was a very disappointing **result**."
6. "We **deserve**d to win!"

A. The fan's team played better than the other team, but the fan's team did not win or draw.
B. The fan expected his team to win, but they didn't.
C. The fan's team were better than the other team for the first 45 minutes: they didn't let the other team have the ball much, and they had the best chances to score.
D. The fan's team played better than the other team, but the fan's team did not win.
E. The score at half-time was 0-3, but the fan's team won 4-3 in the end.
F. The other team passed the ball very quickly, and moved around the pitch very quickly.

Difficulty level 2: "Good to Know"

Ex. 2 These things are said by a television commentator at the end of a game. Match the phrases **in bold** to their *opposites*.

1. "Johnson missed two great chances in the **opening** ten minutes." B
2. "United conceded **late on**, Philips heading in from close range on 88 minutes."
3. "United looked very **nervy** in the second half, but managed to hold on for the win."
4. "This was a **well deserved** victory, United outplayed Wanderers for most of the match."
5. "Despite an **unconvincing** performance, United managed to get the win."

A. lucky
B. final
C. composed

D. impressive
E. early on

Ex. 3 These are things that managers said after matches. Match the words & phrases **in bold** with their explanations:
(Example: 1=B)

"At half-time I said to the lads that we could [1]**turn it around**, we were unlucky to be one-nil down. And they gave me a great performance in the second half. We deserved that win."

"I thought we [2]**outplay**ed them in the first half. But we didn't get the goal, and that cost us, because they had a great second half, and made us pay."

"It was disappointing not to get the win, but you have to **give** the other team [3]**credit** for a fine [4]**display**."

"It wasn't easy, but we [5]**finally** managed to get the goal at the end that I think we deserved."

"It was a [6]**frustrating** afternoon for us. We clearly deserved to win, but the referee clearly didn't want us to!"

"I was pleased because, although we lost, we **show**ed a lot of [7]**spirit** in the second half. There was great effort, and we created a few good chances. We were unlucky not to score."

"It was an [8]**even match**, I think. Both teams could have won it, so I think a draw is a fair result."

A. It was difficult and it took a long time.
B. To come back.
C. Makes you feel a bit angry.
D. How well or badly a team plays.
E. To play enthusiastically and work hard for your team.
F. To play much better than the other team.
G. To praise (say something positive about someone).
H. A match where neither team was dominant.

Ex. 4 Match these sentence halves. The sentences are all from match reports:

1. United managed to **salvage**... E
2. United **struggle**d...
3. It was a **tight**...
4. It got very...
5. Apart from an early **spell**...
6. After going two-nil down early on United were always **chasing the**...
7. United's **defensive**...
8. United **battle**d...
9. The United fans booed the players off after an **abject**...

A. ...game, with chances few and far between.
B. ...of pressure United failed to threaten their opponent's goal.
C. ...**frailties** cost them again, with basic errors leading to the two goals.
D. ...**hard** in the second half but couldn't create any clear chances.
E. ...**a point** with a late equaliser.
F. ...**display**.
G. ...**scrappy** in the second half, with both teams giving the ball away far too easily.
H. ...in the first half and were lucky not to go in one-nil down at the break.
I. ...**game**.

[The phrases **in bold** are defined in the next exercise on the next page]

Ex. 5 These are the sentences from *Ex.4*. Match the phrases **in bold** to their definitions:

1. United managed to **salvage a point** with a late equaliser. *A*
2. United **struggle**d in the first half and were lucky not to go in one-nil down at the break.
3. It was a **tight** game, with chances few and far between.
4. It got very **scrappy** in the second half, with both teams giving the ball away far too easily.
5. Apart from an early **spell** of pressure, United failed to threaten their opponent's goal.
6. After going two-nil down early on United were always **chasing the game**.
7. United's **defensive frailties** cost them again, with basic errors leading to the two goals.
8. United **battle**d **hard** in the second half but couldn't create any clear chances.
9. The United fans booed the players off after an **abject display**.

A. To 'rescue' a draw late in the match, when the team has not really deserved it.
B. A period of a match.
C. A phrase meaning that a team is losing, that they are trying hard to score, and that they are taking risks.
D. To play with a lot of physical effort.
E. Describes a match or a period of a match that is not very beautiful to watch; both teams' passing is not good and they find it difficult to keep the ball and to create flowing combinations.
F. To play badly and therefore risk conceding goals.
G. Weaknesses in the defence of a team.
H. Describes a match or a period of a match where both teams are defending and keeping the ball well, so it is difficult for both teams to score.
I. A really awful performance by a team.

4. ATTACKING

Difficulty level 1: "The Basics"
Ex. 1 Match each sentence with its explanation:

1. United were very successful **breaking down the left**. H
2. United scored **on the counter-attack**.
3. United were very **offensive**.
4. United were effective **on the break**.
5. United's **build-up play** was very **patient**.
6. United's wingers **made** dangerous **runs** down both sides.
7. United were very dangerous **up front**.
8. United's wingers **set up** all the goals.

A. United had attacking tactics.
B. United's midfielders on the left and the right passed the ball so other players could score the goals.
C. United got a goal when they quickly moved the ball from their defence to their attack.
D. United played very well in all attacking areas of the pitch.
E. United's attacking play was good when they moved the ball quickly from their defence to their attack.
F. United's midfielders on the left and the right ran down the sides of the pitch (with, and without, the ball).
G. When united were trying to score a goal they passed the ball and waited for good opportunities, rather than playing the ball quickly towards the goal.
H. United were good when attacking on the left side of the pitch.

Ex. 2 This is part of an article about a team's attacking play. Match the phrases **in bold** with the definitions below:
(Example: 1=A)

"...City's play [1]**in the final third** has been breathtaking at times, and they [2]**look threatening** every time they [3]**press forward**. [4]**Going forward** they have got two attacking full-backs who can [5]**overlap** with their pacey wingers, midfielders who can [6]**arrive late in the box** to contribute to the scoring, and a powerful centre-forward who's able to [7]**run the channels**, [8]**lead the line** and [9]**poach goals**. The manager is clearly fundamentally [10]**attack minded** and puts out sides designed to penetrate and [11]**break down defences**..."

These match with 1-6:
A. In the part of the pitch nearest to the opponent's goal.
B. Attacking.
C. (Starting in a position quite far back) to run into the area around the goal to try and score, but waiting until the last moment so it is difficult for the defenders to mark you.
D. To run in front of the player on your own team who plays in the position in front of you (usually on the sides of the pitch).
E. To attack strongly.
F. To play in a way which means the team has a good chance of scoring.

These match with 7-11:
G. To play as an attacker who plays the furthest up the pitch. This player receives long balls and holds the ball in order to give other players time to join the attack.
H. To have the ability to score goals with a simple kick or header because the player's positional play is so good (he is able to be in the right place at the right time).
I. To patiently get through the defence of the other team with intelligent passing and movement.
J. To make attacking runs (without the ball) in the spaces between the defenders (the player hopes that he will get a pass or create space for other players on his team).
K. Describing a person who thinks offensive play, rather than defensive play, is most important.

Difficulty level 3: "Advanced"
Ex. 3 These sentences are from television commentaries. Match the synonyms below to the words and phrases **in bold**:

1. "Patterson is **bomb**ing down the wing." F
2. "Russel **popp**ed **up** at the back post to head it in."
3. "That was a dangerous ball **over the top** from James."
4. "Wanderers haven't managed to exploit the **gap**s in Albion's defence."
5. "That was an excellent **drive** down the left from Murphy."
6. "Albion are really **hav**ing **a go at them** now."
7. "Bell **pick**ed **up** the ball on the halfway line."
8. "Wanderers have managed to survive the **onslaught** so far."
9. "Both the wingers' **final ball** has been poor tonight."

A. over the defence
B. (to) attack strongly
C. (to) appear
D. attacking run (with the ball)
E. passes to the strikers (so they can score)
F. (to) sprint
G. hole
H. (to) get
I. constant attacking

Ex. 4 These are sentences from match reports. Can you guess what the words and phrases **in bold** mean?

...after going behind early to a penalty, City were always **chasing the game**...
...United were **chasing the game** and left holes at the back...
...Rovers were **chasing the game** and switched to a more attacking 4-4-2...

...he **cut in** from the left and fired a shot low past the keeper...
...the keeper dived high to his right to save Peter's powerful shot after the No 6 **cut in** from the right...
...Davis **cut in** from the left to send in a cross from which Stevens looped a header inches over...

...Etherington's goal was **under siege** for the whole of the second half, but somehow Albion failed to score...
...after the break Wanderers came out and put Rovers' goal **under siege**, getting their reward on 70 minutes with a fine goal...
...Neil Simmon's side were **under siege** for much of the first half and were lucky not to go behind...

...United were left free to pass the ball around the edge of the penalty area but failed to **find an opening**...
...City finally managed to **find an opening** when Brown exploited a rare gap in their opponent's defence to play Richards in on goal...
...although the central-defensive partnership was impressive throughout, Bailey managed to **find an opening** with 10 minutes left to play...

5. Defending

Ex. 1 Match each sentence with its explanation. Smith is on team A and Williams is on team B:

1. Smith **pass**ed the ball **out of defence**. *C*
2. Smith **put** Williams **under pressure**.
3. Smith **block**ed Williams' shot.
4. Smith **mark**ed Williams for the whole game.
5. Smith **left** Williams **unmarked**.
6. Smith **clear**ed the ball.
7. Smith **tackle**d Williams.

A. Williams tried to score a goal, but Smith stopped the ball travelling towards the goal.
B. Smith followed Williams and tried to make sure that he didn't get the ball.
C. Smith tried to give the ball to another player on his team, he didn't just kick it away.
D. Smith didn't follow Williams, so it was easy for Williams to get the ball.
E. Smith went close to Williams, who had the ball, so Williams didn't have much time to think, or to control the ball.
F. Smith took the ball away from Williams.
G. The ball was in a dangerous area, so Smith kicked it away.

Ex. 2 This is part of a manager's half-time team talk. He's not happy with his team's defending. Use what he says to fill the gaps in the words & phrases which are explained below:

"...What happened for the first goal? He was **unmarked** at the far post! Jenson—that was your man. You've got to concentrate more! We need to keep our shape—don't let them drag you out of position. If your man tries to drag you out of position, then pass him on to someone else, and pick up another man instead. You need to communicate more.

We're letting them shoot too easily from the edge of the box. Don't back off, make a challenge. Close the player down!

We're playing far too deep. Push up a bit, communicate, and play the offside trap.

We're supposed to be playing a flat back-four today, but it doesn't look like it! You've got to concentrate and move up and down together to hold the line.

Brown, stay on your feet! You've got a yellow card already and you were luckily not to get another. No more sliding tackles, unless it's absolutely necessary. We can't afford to go down to ten men!

And if both centre-backs go up for a corner, organise yourselves! Someone needs to cover them..."

1. A player has no defender near him. So it was easy for him to get the ball. We can say he is... : _unmarked_
2. Player A moves into another area of the pitch and takes player B (from the other team) with him. Player B is now in the wrong position. We can say player B has been... : **dragged** _____
3. A synonym phrase for 'tackle'... : **make a** _____
4. A synonym phrase for 'pressurise a player'... : _____ **a player down**
5. The defence of team A works together to try and get players from team B offside. We can say team A is... : **playing an offside** _____
6. The defence has four players and they work together in a straight line. We call this... : **playing a** _____
7. The type of tackle where a player slides along the ground... : _____
8. To go into another player's position for a short time while this player is not in his normal position. _____

Football English

Ex. 3 This is a list of word combinations with the word 'tackle'. Match each one to its definition below:

1. A fair tackle *A*
2. A two-footed tackle
3. A dangerous tackle
4. A well-timed tackle
5. A 50-50 tackle
6. A late tackle
7. A mistimed tackle

A. A tackle that probably involves physical contact, but is not a foul.
B. The defender makes his tackle at exactly the right time.
C. The defender makes his tackle too early or too late, so he fouls the other player.
D. A tackle which could injure the other player.
E. The other player has already passed the ball when the defender makes the tackle.
F. The defender jumps and uses both of his feet to win the ball.
G. A tackle where both players have an equal chance of getting the ball when they decide to make the tackle.

Ex. 4 This is part of a television post-match analysis. The pundit is criticising the losing team's defending. Find the words & phrases which are explained below:

"...So, if we pause the action here... this is a good example of their poor defending today. First of all, they're **defending** much too **high up** the pitch. They're playing a dangerous game; relying on the off-side trap...[action continues]

...A simple, long-ball from Evans, and a well-timed run from Patrick, can now totally split the defence. They're not the quickest central-defensive partnership, and Boothe has to be much tighter to Patrick here. It's much too easy for Evans to pick him out, and all he has to do is beat the keeper. It's their defensive frailties that have lost them this match, they really need to be more solid at the back...[action continues]

...Here we can see some more basic defensive errors. Boothe can just shield the ball and let it go out of play. But he decides to turn with it in a dangerous area, and loses it. And then Wilson is caught sleeping, he isn't goalside, which means it's easy for Patrick to get a shot in. It's easy to see why they haven't kept a clean sheet yet this season..."

1. If the line of defenders should be further back, we can say they are... : _defending too high up_
2. If an attacking pass finds a lot space between the defenders, we can say it... : _____
3. The two players who play in the middle of defence are a... : _____
4. If a defender is close to an attacking player, we can say he is... : _____
5. The weak aspects of a team's defending can be called its... : _____
6. A synonym for 'in defence'... : _____
7. To protect the ball with your body strength... : _____
8. When defending, to be on the correct side of the player you are marking... : _____

Ex. 5 Fill the gaps in the phrases **in bold**. Then match the phrases to their explanations:

A. solid

B. ~~making~~

C. won

D. zonal

1. United were lucky there, Wright _making_ **a goal-line clearance.** *B/ii*
2. The referee made a mistake there. The replay clearly shows he _____ **the ball cleanly.**
3. The manager has switched to a _____ **marking system** to try and sort out their defensive problems.
4. United have got a _____ **defence** this season.

i. A good defence.
ii. When standing in the goal, the defender prevents a goal by kicking the ball away.
iii. To successfully tackle without making a foul.
iv. A system of defending where defenders are not responsible for particular players on the other team, but for areas of the pitch.

Difficulty level 3: "Advanced"
Ex. 6 (This is the same type of exercise as *Ex. 5*). Fill the gaps in the phrases **in bold**. Then match the phrases to their explanations:

A. defensive   D. pressing
B. all   E. lunge
C. pick

1. Rovers were often able to regain possession very quickly with their _____ **game**.
2. He received a red card for a **two-footed** _____ on Sanders in the 88th minute.
3. Their defensive line was _____ **over the place** in the first half.
4. His movement is so good that it is difficult for defenders to _____ **him up**.
5. They score lots of goals, but it's their _____ **record** which is the problem.

i. A tactic: when a team has lost the ball they make a big effort to get it back again as soon as possible by putting a lot of pressure on the other team.
ii. The statistics which show how many goals other teams have scored against a team.
iii. Following a player on the other team to try and make sure that he doesn't get the ball.
iv. Very disorganised.
v. A strong, quick, stretching tackle. The tackler doesn't have much control, and so it is potentially dangerous.

Ex. 7 (This is the same type of exercise as *Ex.5* & *6*). Fill the gaps in the phrases **in bold**. Then match the phrases to their explanations:

A. stem   C. ditch

B. drop   D. early

1. I think Johnson **committed too** _____ there. He could have just stood up and waited for some others to get back and help him.

2. After the sending off Carlson will have to _____ **back into defence.**

3. Hall **made** a fantastic **last-** _____ **tackle** to prevent an equalising goal.

4. United have been under a lot of pressure this half, but have managed to _____ **the tide**, and will be happy with the 0-0 at half-time.

i. When a player who normally doesn't play in defence switches to playing in defence.

ii. To stop another player from scoring at the last moment.

iii. To successfully defend a long period of attacking by the other team.

iv. To make a tackle too soon.

6. TACTICS

Ex. 1 Match these tactical concepts with the situations:

1. pressing D
2. possession
3. movement
4. width

5. positioning
6. a high-line
7. shape

A. "...United passed accurately and kept the ball well..."
B. "...Winters left lots of space at the back by coming too far up the pitch..."
C. "...Albion were very organised and got back into their formation quickly when they lost the ball..."
D. "...Rovers were given no time on the ball and were very quickly closed down in midfield..."
E. "...Wanderers were very difficult to mark going forward and always created two or three passing options for the man on the ball..."
F. "...City were far too narrow with both wide men always choosing to come inside rather than exploit the space on the wings..."
G. "...at times United's back four were almost defending from the half-way line..."

Ex. 2 This is part of a half-time television analysis. Find the words & phrases which are described below:

"...Rovers have **put out** quite **a defensive side** today. They're allowing City to **dominate possession** and are hoping to catch them on the break. When they're attacking, they're being very **direct**, getting the ball up to the lone striker as quickly as possible with long balls. City are trying to **create space** in the middle by directing play down the two wings, but are finding this quite difficult as the Rovers' midfield are pressing well; **closing down** the City midfield immediately. City have caused Rovers the most problems when they've managed to **switch the play** from one wing to the other quickly. Osbourn is also having some success in his **free role**; managing to find a bit of space in some dangerous positions..."

1. To move into an area of the pitch in order to make more room in another area of the pitch... : _(to) create space_

2. To keep the ball much more than the other team... : _____

3. To play a negative formation; designed to stop the other side scoring rather than creating attacking play... : _____

4. A synonym for pressing (a team/player)... : _____

5. Describes a style of play which involves attacking with long balls played quickly towards the goal rather than short, patient passing... : _____

6. The job of moving around into different attacking areas rather than staying strictly in one position... : _____

7. To move the ball quickly from one side of the pitch to the other... : _____

Ex. 3 These are things said by managers during the half-time team talk. Match them with the situations:

1. "We need to **drop deep**er in defence." *C*
2. "We need to **play it short**."
3. "We need to **track** his runs."
4. "We need to **exploit the space** in the **wide areas**."
5. "We need to **work as a unit**."

A. An attacking player from the other team is getting a lot of space in some dangerous positions.
B. There's a **lack of width** when attacking.
C. The other team are managing to make passes **in behind** the defensive line.
D. **Long balls** to the centre forward are unsuccessful.
E. The defence is not organised and not moving up and down the pitch together.

Ex. 4 (This exercise is the same type as *Ex.3*) These are things said by managers during the half-time team talk. Match them with the situations:

1. "We need to **make a change** and **bring on** an extra man in the middle."
2. "We need to change our **game plan**."
3. "We need to be more **compact**."
4. "We need to **go route one** more often."

A. The other team is finding lots of space between the defenders and midfield.
B. The current strategy is not working.
C. Patient attacking isn't working, a more direct style is required.
D. The other team is dominating in midfield.

Football English

Ex. 5 These sentences are from match reports. Choose the correct alternatives for the parts **in bold**:

1. Rovers **made a like-for-like replacement** at half-time. D
2. Rovers had **a spare man** in midfield.
3. Rovers tried to **take the game to United** in the second half.
4. Rovers' **ball retention was very good**.
5. Rovers managed to **stretch the play**.
6. Rovers **sat deep**.

A. had most of the possession
B. create space in the centre by exploiting the wide areas
C. an extra player
D. substituted an attacker for another attacker
E. got lots of players behind the ball very quickly when they lost possession, and defended far back
F. be positive and take some risks when attacking

Ex. 6 (This exercise is the same type as *Ex.5*) These sentences are from match reports. Choose the correct alternatives for the parts **in bold**:

1. Rovers gave their star player **licence to roam**.
2. Rovers had a **numerical advantage** after Cooke was sent off.
3. Rovers **made an enforced change** at half-time.
4. Rovers were very successful down the **flanks**.
5. Rovers found space **in between the lines**.
6. Rovers managed to **close out the game** in the second half.

A. in the area between the opposition's midfield and defence
B. wings
C. an extra player
D. a free role
E. protect their lead by not taking risks when attacking
F. had to replace the injured Jennings

7. THE RULES & THE REFEREE

Difficulty level 1: "The Basics"

Ex. 1 Match the list of decisions that a referee can make with the possible situations:

1. A free kick *B*
2. A penalty (kick)
3. A throw-in
4. A goal kick

5. A corner (kick)
6. A kick off
7. A drop/dropped ball

A. A goalkeeper saves a shot and pushes the ball over the line behind the goal.
B. A player pushes his opponent in the back while tackling him.
C. A goal is scored.
D. A player shoots and misses, the ball goes over the line behind the goal.
E. The play has to stop for a few minutes because a fan has run on the pitch.
F. A player is fouled inside the large square around the goal.
G. The ball goes over a line at the side of the pitch.

Difficulty level 1: "The Basics"

Ex. 2 Match these fouls to their pictures:

1. A push in the back *C*
2. A trip
3. Shirt pulling

4. Handball
5. A dive
6. Time-wasting

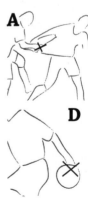
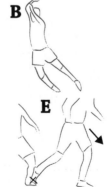
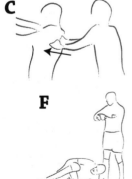

Ex. 3 Put the sentences in the right order, and match them to the situation:

1. The referee for gave handball a free kick
   The referee gave a free kick for handball / D
2. The referee half-time the whistle blew for
3. The referee booked a bad tackle him for
4. The referee him sent dangerous play off for
5. The referee the played advantage

A. Forty-five minutes had already been played.
B. A player on team A was fouled, but the referee let play continue as this was better for team A.
C. A player got a yellow card.
D. A player controlled the ball with his arm.
E. A player got a red card.

Difficulty level 2: "Good to Know"
Ex. 4 These are things said by fans while they are watching a game. Match the sentence halves, then choose the correct situation:

1. "That was a **deliberate**... *D/iv*   A. ...**for offside**."
2. "The linesman's **flag**ging...   B. ...**contact** with him!"
3. "I can't believe the referee...
4. "We always concede   C. ...**suspension**."
   from **dead-ball**...   D. ...**handball**!"
5. "He didn't even **make**...
6. "Great! That means he gets   E. ...**situations**!"
   an **automatic**...   F. ...didn't **spot** that!"

i. The referee hasn't seen a foul.
ii. The referee's assistant is signalling to the referee.
iii. The referee has given a penalty but he has been tricked; a player has simulated being fouled.
iv. A player has intentionally controlled the ball with his arm.
v. The referee has given a player a yellow card. This means that the player will not be able to play in the next match.
vi. The fan's team have conceded a goal from a corner or a free kick.

Ex. 5 Match these synonyms:

1.	The linesman *D*	A.	A suspension
2.	To show a red card	B.	To give a spot-kick
3.	To award a penalty	C.	To rule out a goal
4.	A ban	D.	The assistant referee
5.	To show a yellow card	E.	A dismissal
6.	A red card	F.	To send off
7.	To disallow a goal	G.	To caution

Difficulty level 2: "Good to Know"
Ex. 6 Match these sentence halves. All the sentences are from match reports:

1. ...but the ref clearly **miss**ed... *D*
2. ...his first yellow card came when he **was booked**...
3. ...all the United players **claim**ed...
4. ...Jones' complaining became too much for the ref and he **was booked**...
5. ...all the United players **protest**ed...
6. ...Robson received a yellow card for **kicking**...
7. ...replays showed that the assistant referee was correct and Thompson was indeed **in an offside**...
8. ...the referee gave an **indirect**...

A.   ...**against** the ref's decision, but to no avail.
     [They said that the referee was wrong]
B.   ...**a penalty**, but the referee was unmoved.
     [They said they should have had a penalty]
C.   ...**free kick** inside the box for dangerous play.
     [A goal couldn't be scored from the free kick without it touching another player first]
D.   ...**the incident**, otherwise he would have surely sent him off.
     [He didn't see something important, e.g. a foul or a player pushing another player]
E.   ...**position** when the ball was played.
F.   ...**for dissent**. *[The player complained too strongly to the referee in a disrespectful way]*
G.   ...**for his celebration**; jumping into the fans and removing his shirt.
H.   ...**the ball away**.

Ex. 7 These sentences are from match reports or match commentaries. Can you guess what the words & phrases **in bold** mean?

...already **on a booking**, Collins lunged at the Wanderers' striker, Price, and left the referee with no choice but to issue a second yellow card...

...he was fortunate not to be sent off for tripping Walker when already **on a booking**...

...Sullivan, who is already **on a booking**, is lucky to stay on the field after wiping Porter out with a reckless sliding tackle...

...that's a yellow card for Dixon for **a tug** on Knight's shirt right on the edge of the area...

...Harper gives away a free kick for **a tug** on the hand of Williamson just outside the City penalty area...

...he probably wouldn't have reached the ball, and the keeper would probably have got there first, but Lowe gave him **a tug** just to make sure...

...the Albion players complained that the **infringement** was outside the box...

...Bates found the back of the net but the referee had already blown up for an earlier **infringement**...

...Baldwin clearly made contact with a hand, but at such close range the referee saw no **infringement**...

...the referee and his assistant were not popular with the home fans after a decision to **penalise** Yates for deliberate handball and award United a penalty...

...as the ball is crossed the whistle goes to **penalise** some pushing inside the area...

...The Rovers' manager is incensed that the referee failed to **penalise** Atkins' challenge on Bond inside the penalty area...

...After the match the United manager complained that they had two **stonewall penalties** turned down...

..."It was a **stonewall penalty**," said Hutchinson. "The defender left his leg out and tripped him."...

... "It was a **stonewall penalty**," complained Winters afterwards. "He took me down. No question."...

...Wanderers face being disqualified from the competition for fielding **ineligible** players...

...Their new Brazilian striker was **ineligible** to play while they await his work permit...

...Benton was **ineligible** as he has already played in this season's Champions League for his former club...

Ex. 8 This is an extract from a match report. Find the words & phrases which are explained below:

"...it was a very busy match for the referee Paul Franks who had to **point to the spot** on three occasions, as well as turning down numerous other penalty appeals. The first spot-kick was awarded to Athletic when Carver clipped McDonald just inside the area. Replays were inconclusive, but showed, at most, that limited contact was made. The Rovers supporters certainly felt it was a very soft penalty decision and were incensed. However the referee could soon make amends a few minutes later by sending Reilly off for a second bookable offence and giving a penalty Rovers' way as punishment for a needless deliberate-handball in the box. Just before the half-time whistle Rovers had another good penalty shout. Slater appeared to bring down Irwin, but this time Franks was unwilling to make a decision, perhaps because of a poor view of the incident in a crowded penalty area..."

1. A phrase meaning that the referee gives a penalty... : _point to the spot_
2. When a team asks the referee for a penalty... : _____
3. A synonym for a penalty... : _____
4. When a player makes another player fall over by lightly touching the player's foot as he runs past... : _____
5. A penalty that was not a very clear penalty... : _____
6. A foul, or another infringement, which the referee can give a yellow card for... : _____
7. A situation when there is a chance that the referee will give a penalty for your team... : _____
8. A situation where the referee has to make a decision... : _____

8. THE SCORE & RESULTS

Difficulty level 1: "The Basics"

Ex. 1 Match this list of scores to the sentences below. Rovers are the home team:

1. 6-0
2. 0-0
3. 4-0
4. 0-4
5. 1-1
6. 1-0 A

A. "Rovers **won one-nil**."
B. "Rovers **drew one all**."
C. "It was a **scoreless draw**."
D. "Rovers' **four-nil victory** was well deserved."
E. "Rovers' **four-nil defeat** was their worst performance of the season so far."
F. "Rovers **thrash**ed them!"

Difficulty level 2: "Good to Know"

Ex. 2 This is an extract from a match report. Find the phrases which are defined below:

"...Albion will be the happier of the two teams after **coming from behind** to earn a one-all draw and taking a much needed point from a difficult away fixture. 'We deserved that draw. It was important for us to get a result here today,' the manager said, and few would disagree with his assessment. At one-nil down it looked like they had a mountain to climb. City had scored after a period of sustained pressure and didn't look like they were going to take their foot off the gas. Incisive attacking play created three more clear chances before the half-hour mark, and at this stage no one would have bet on it finishing one-one. However, Albion remained calm and organised, and by the break they were unlucky to still be behind..."

1. To get a win or a draw even though at one point in the match the other team was winning... : _to come from behind_
2. To get a draw or a win... : _____
3. A phrase which means: 'when the score was 1-0'... : _____
4. A phrase which means: 'the final score is 1-1'... : _____
5. To be losing... : _____

Ex. 3 Fill in the gaps in the sentences from match reports below. Use these definitions to help you:

A shock result: a final score that nobody expected.

An upset: a final score that nobody expected.

A convincing win: when the team that wins dominates the match.

A rout: when one team scores a lot more goals than the other.

To register a win: to win (normally used in writing rather than speaking).

1. "City have caused a few _upsets_ this season by beating three of last season's top-four this campaign, but were unable to beat the favourites for the Championship today."

2. "Harrison completed the _____ with a sixth goal in injury time."

3. "Given Wanderers' poor form of late, this win was definitely the shock _____ of the day."

4. "United produced a _____ win today, their goal was never really under threat."

5. "Rovers _____ their first win of the season, coming out on top of a tight battle."

9. Scoring Goals

Difficulty level 1: "The Basics"
Ex. 1 Match these phrases with their explanations:

1. to score an own goal *C*
2. to get the equaliser
3. to concede a goal
4. to get the winner
5. to score a hat trick
6. to take a deflection into the net

A. A player scores the goal which means his team wins.
B. A player scores, but the ball changes direction just before it goes into the goal because it hits another player.
C. A player scores a goal for the *other* team by mistake.
D. A player scores 3 goals in one match.
E. A player scores a goal which means both teams now have the same number of goals.
F. A team lets the other team score a goal.

Difficulty level 1: "The Basics"
Ex. 2 These sentences are said by fans watching matches on television. Fill in the gaps (with words from *Ex.1*):

A. concede   C. deflection
B. ~~own~~   D. equaliser

1. "It was really unlucky! The defender tackled the striker but **score**d an _own_ goal at the same time!" *B*
2. "It's 2-2 now. Richards **got** the _____ ."
3. "Typical! Rovers can't defend corners, they _____ **a goal** every game from a corner".
4. "That was unlucky! The shot wasn't very good, but it **took** a _____ and went through the keeper's legs!"

Ex. 3 These are sentences from match reports describing goal scoring. Fill in the gaps:

A. behind   F. for
B. on   G. front
C. from   H. against
D. ~~with~~   I. of
E. in

- The defender scored [1] _with_ his left foot [2]_____ 32 minutes.
- Robinson got a late winner [3]_____ the home side [4]_____ the 89th minute.
- This was the first time he had scored [5] _____ Rovers, and only his fifth goal [6] _____ the season.
- They went in [7]_____ after only 3 minutes, the goal coming [8]_____ a free kick on the edge of the area.
- The away team never looked like equalising after going [9]_____ early on.

Ex. 4 Match the phrases with their explanations:

1. score from the spot **E**
2. score a well-deserved goal
3. score a consolation goal
4. score on the counter attack
5. score a goal against the run of play

A. The goal was not important because it came near the end, and the other team already had enough goals.
B. The goal was scored by a team in a period of the match when the other team was playing better.
C. The goal was scored when the team stopped an attack by the other team and then quickly attacked themselves.
D. The goal was scored by the team who was playing the best.
E. The goal was scored from a penalty kick.

Ex. 5 For each score change below choose the correct sentence:

[3–0 = team A have three goals, team B have no goals]

1. 0 – 0 ➔ 1 – 0
   a) "Team A have **taken the lead**!" ✓
   b) "Team A have **equalise**d!"

2. 0 – 0 ➔ 0 – 1
   a) "Team A have **opened the scoring**!"
   b) "Team B have **opened the scoring**!"

3. 1 – 0 ➔ 2 – 0
   a) "Team A have **restored their lead**!"
   b) "Have A have **doubled their lead**!"

4. 1 – 2 ➔ 1 – 3
   a) " Team B have **taken the lead**!"
   b) "Team B have **extended their lead**!"

5. 1 – 0 ➔ 1 – 1 ➔ 2 – 1
   a) "Team A have **restored their lead**!"
   b) "Team B have **restored their lead**!"

6. 1 – 2 ➔ 2 – 2
   a) "Team A have **drawn level**!"
   b) "Team A have **opened the scoring**!"

7. 0 – 0 ➔ 0 – 1
   a) "Team A have **gone ahead**!"
   b) "Team B have **gone ahead**!"

8. 0 – 2 ➔ 1 – 2 ➔ 2 – 2
   a) "Team B have **come back from** two–nil **down**!"
   b) "Team A have **come back from** two–nil **down**!"

Ex. 6 This is an extract from a match report. Find the words & phrases which are explained below:

"...It was Stevens' **assist** that allowed Dooley to score the opener just before the break. Showing the confidence and composure that he has often lacked this season Dooley finished calmly after waiting for the keeper to make the first move. Stevens was also the provider for City's second when he set up Richards on the edge of the box with a perfectly weighted pass. The thunderous shot was saved well by Atkins in the Wanderers' goal, but Richards was quick to slot home from the rebound..."

1. The pass or cross to the player who scores is an... : _assist_

2. If a player doesn't panic when he gets the ball and thinks calmly about what to do with it then he shows... : _____

3. To make the final kick into the net to score a goal... : _____

4. To pass or cross to another player so he can score... : _____

5. To score when the ball comes off the post or crossbar, or when the keeper saves but doesn't catch the ball, is to **score from the**... : _____

Ex. 7 Match the sentence halves:

1. Rovers drew level with a somewhat **lucky**... *G*
2. Walters could only **turn the ball into**...
3. Bradley scored to give City **a two goal**...
4. Pemberton arrived late in the box to meet Chambers' cross for **an** easy **tap**...
5. Samson calmly **picked his**...
6. Morris should have **put it**...
7. That was a **soft**...
8. The **decisive**...

A. ...**goal**; United will be very unhappy with some poor defending there.
B. ...**cushion**.
C. ...**spot** to beat the keeper at the far post.
D. ...**goal** came in the 65th minute, when Taylor finally managed to find some space in the United defence and give Wanderers the lead.
E. ...**his own net**.
F. ...**in** to bring the score level.
G. ...**goal**.
H. ...**away** easily but could only shoot straight at the keeper.

[The phrases **in bold** are defined in the next exercise]

Ex. 8 These are the sentences from *Ex.7*. Match the phrases **in bold** with their definitions:

1. Rovers drew level with a somewhat **lucky goal**. *A*
2. Walters could only **turn the ball into his own net**.
3. Bradley scored to give City **a two goal cushion**.
4. Pemberton arrived late in the box to meet Chambers' cross for **an easy tap in** to bring the score level.
5. Samson calmly **picked his spot** to beat the keeper at the far post.
6. Morris should have **put it away** easily but could only shoot straight at the keeper.
7. That was a **soft goal**; United will be very unhappy with some poor defending there.
8. The **decisive goal** came in the 65th minute, when Taylor finally managed to find some space in the United defence and give Wanderers the lead.

A. A goal that a team were fortunate to score.
B. A goal that a team could score easily, the other team probably made a big mistake.
C. A very important goal (in the context of this match).
D. A lead of more than one goal, so the team in the lead can relax a bit.
E. To score an own goal.
F. To score.
G. A goal which is easy for the player to score, he is near the goal, doesn't need to kick the ball hard, and the goalkeeper is not in a good position.
H. To score by guiding the ball into an area which the keeper cannot reach, rather than shooting with great power.

10. SHOOTING

Difficulty level 2: "Good to Know"
Ex. 1 These sentences are said by fans during a match just after a player shoots unsuccessfully at goal. Match the sentences to the situations below:

1. "He should have **hit it first time**!" D
2. "He's got to at least **hit the target**!"
3. "He tried to **place it** but he should have gone for power!"
4. "That was a very **tight angle**!"
5. "That was awful **finishing**!"

A. The player didn't even make the goalkeeper save the ball because his shot missed the goal completely.

B. The player had a chance but his attempt to score was very bad.

C. It was very difficult for the player to score because he was not in front of the goal, but far off to the side of the goal.

D. The player didn't shoot immediately but controlled the ball first before he shot.

E. The player's intention was to shoot the ball carefully and accurately (into an area of the goal which would make it very difficult for the goalkeeper to make a save).

Ex. 2 These sentences are from match reports. Fill in the gaps. Use the definitions below to help you:

A strike: a shot (which often results in a goal).

To fire in: to shoot powerfully.

Back-lift: the movement that the player makes with his kicking foot just before he kicks the ball.

A snap shot: a shot for which the player doesn't have much time to prepare, the shot is an instinctive reaction.

To scuff a shot: to shoot, but the player doesn't make contact with the ball cleanly; he kicks the ground at the same time as the ball so the shot is less powerful than intended.

To slot home: to shoot and score after receiving a pass. Often the shot is along the ground, the player doesn't need to control the ball first, and it is quite easy to score because the goalkeeper is out of position.

1. "Albion broke quickly down the left with Cox finding Mason free on the penalty spot who **slot**ted _home_ easily."

2. "A late _____ from Fielding earned Rovers a draw."

3. "Roberts _____ in a shot low and hard from just outside the box."

4. "The keeper was deceived by the very short _____ and wasn't ready for the shot."

5. "A great chance fell to Lewis but he _____ his **shot** and the ball rolled harmlessly to the keeper."

11. Skills & Abilities

Difficulty level 1: "The Basics"
Ex. 1 Fill the gaps in the sentences with these words & phrases:

A. pace	E. tactically disciplined
B. two-footed	F. technical ability
C. close control	G. go past players
D. playmaker	H. defensively disciplined

1. He's _two-footed_ : *He is good with his left and right boot.*

2. He can _____ : *He is able to take the ball past players who are trying to tackle him.*

3. He's got great _____ : *He's very quick.*

4. He's got a lot of _____ : *His technique is very good.*

5. His _____ is excellent : *E.g. he is very good at stopping the ball if it is passed to him, or keeping the ball at his feet while he is running.*

6. He's the _____ : *He is a very creative player whose job is to create attacking opportunities, e.g. by making difficult passes through the other team's defence.*

7. He is very _____ : *He understands his responsibilities to help stop the other team scoring, and doesn't take unnecessary risks when attacking.*

8. He is very _____ : *He understands his responsibilities in the team's system.*

Ex. 2 Match this list of football skills with their pictures & definitions:

1. A step over *E/iii*   4. A nutmeg
2. A drag back   5. An overhead/scissor kick
3. A backheel

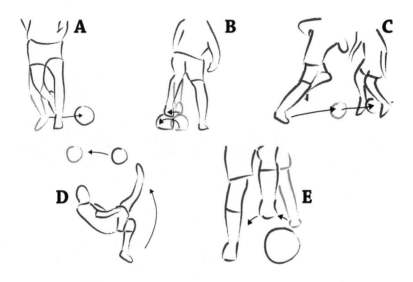

i. The player kicks the ball through an opponent's legs.

ii. The ball is in the air. The player jumps and kicks the ball in the air in a backwards direction.

iii. The player moves *like* he is going to kick the ball, but his foot goes over the ball and he doesn't touch the ball.

iv. The player passes the ball with the back of his boot.

v. The player puts his boot on the top of the ball and rolls the ball backwards.

Ex. 3 These sentences describe players' strengths. Match the sentence halves & the explanations:

1. He's very good **in**... *C/ii*	A. ...**the game** is excellent.
2. He's very...	B. ...**ball specialist**.
3. He's **a ball**...	C. ...**the air**.
4. He shows great...	D. ...**winner**.
5. He's a **dead**...	E. ...**versatile**.
6. His **ability to read**...	F. ...**leadership** on the pitch.

i. He is a midfield player who is very good at tackling.

ii. He can head the ball very well.

iii. He's very good at taking free kicks.

iv. He can anticipate what other players will do very well.

v. He can play in a variety of positions.

vi. He is respected by his teammates, and makes them feel confident by encouraging and helping them in difficult situations.

Ex. 4 A manager has just signed two new players and is telling the press about them. Find the phrases that are defined below in his comments:

Player 1:

"He's very good at **shielding**, and holding up the ball until others can join the attack. But he's also got a burst of pace which scares defenders. His work-rate is also good, which is important, as everyone in this team has to press when we don't have possession."

(These phrases can be found in the comments about Player 1:)

1. How much physical effort a player makes... : _____
2. Protecting the ball with your body to stop an opponent getting it... : *shielding*
3. To be able to run very fast over short distances... : _____
4. Keeping possession of the ball in an attacking position (without passing it) because there is no other player available to pass to yet... : _____

Player 2:

"He's a midfielder, but he's very versatile; he's played at left and centre back in the past, so he'll be a useful utility player in the squad. He covers a lot of ground as well. An area for improvement is perhaps goalscoring; I'd like to see him develop into a box-to-box midfielder, and contribute about 10 goals a season for us."

(These phrases can be found in the comments about Player 2:)

5. To run a lot during a match... : _____
6. A player who is flexible and can play in various positions if the manager needs him to... : _____
7. A midfielder who is good at defending, attacking and scoring goals... : _____

Ex. 5 These are things a television commentator says during a match. Match the words & phrases **in bold** with their definitions:

1. "That pass showed great **vision** from Payne." *ii*

2. "The defender had no chance, he absolutely **skin**ned **him**!"

3. "What a great **dummy** from Gardner, fooling two defenders and creating space behind for Sims to run into."

4. "He fooled the defender by **feint**ing one way then the other."

5. "A **teasing run** into the box and a powerful shot brings a good save from the keeper."

6. "A **surging run** takes Reid past two defenders, but the resulting shot is disappointing."

i. Running with the ball very quickly.

ii. The ability to be able to think creatively and see opportunities for unexpected passes.

iii. To move *like* you will receive a pass, but then you leave the ball so a teammate can get it.

iv. To move *like* you will kick the ball or change direction, but then you do not, in order to trick your opponent.

v. To run much faster than your opponent who is also running to get the ball.

vi. Dribbling with the ball and changing direction frequently.

12. MANAGEMENT & SIGNINGS

Difficulty level 1: "The Basics"
Ex. 1 (Use the list of definitions below to help you with this exercise) Fill the gaps in these comments made by television commentators during matches:

The **manager**: the person responsible for coaching the team, choosing the team and buying and selling players. Normally used to talk about people working in the British game.

The **coach**: the person responsible for choosing and coaching the team (but with less responsibility for buying and selling players than a manager).

To **fire** a manager: to tell a manager he has to leave his job.

To **appoint** a manager: to give a (new) manager a job.

A **team talk**: when a manager or coach instructs his players about tactics and tries to motivate them. It can be before a match or at half-time.

The **chairman**: the person who officially has overall control of a football club. Normally used to talk about the British game. In other countries this may be the 'president'.

The **board**: the group of people who officially have control of a football club.

To **sign a player**: to buy a (new) player.

To **sign a player on loan**: to get a player who belongs to another team to play for you for a short period.

A **transfer fee**: the amount of money one club pays another club to get a new player.

A **scout**: a person whose job it is to find out information about possible new players.

Wages: the amount of money paid to a player by the club. The sum is normally given per week in Britain.

The **transfer window**: a period when clubs are allowed to buy players from each other.

A **contract**: the document which contains the details of the agreement between a player and the club about wages and how long they will stay etc.

. "United's second-half performance has been much improved, the manager's half-time [1] *team talk* must have had some effect."
. "The manager will be looking forward to the summer [2]_____ when he can invest in some new players."
. "The left-back joined Albion [3]_____ loan in January because of their defensive injury crisis."
. "Evan's joined for a club record ten-million [4]_____, so he's under a lot of pressure to perform."
. "There was good news this week after Wanderers announced that they are going to build a new stadium after a [5]_____ meeting on Wednesday."
. "He was [6]_____ in January, so this is only the manager's third match in charge."

Ex. 2 This is an extract from a newspaper interview with a new manager. Read the interview and find the words and phrases which are defined below:

*Has the chairman given you a **transfer budget** to sign any new players?*

We'll be signing some new players in the summer definitely. But there's no fixed transfer budget. It depends who's available. We're going to strengthen the squad, and if the right players are available at the right price, they'll be signed. The funds are there.

Do you have any transfer targets in mind?

Yes, of course. But I'm not going to tell you who of course! Nice try.

And have you got the necessary funds to meet the wage demands of the top players you'll need to strengthen your squad?

Yes. We can pay top wages here, to get the top talent. We just need to make sure that the transfer fees are reasonable. If we can plan carefully and pay low transfer fees, maybe even sign a player or two on a free transfer, then we'll be able to use the money we save on fees to pay the kind of wages that the top players are demanding these days.

And what kind of wages would that be?

Well it's no secret what our players are getting paid. Top players are receiving eighty to a hundred thousand a week* in this league. We have to pay those kind of wages if we're to compete at this level.

There have been rumours that Sampson will be leaving this summer. His contract runs out at the end of next season...

Well, you said it, a rumour. Sampson is committed to the club, and we plan to open contract negotiations with him in the close season. We're confident that he'll sign a new, long term, contract extension.

You haven't brought any of your old back-room staff with you from United. Will some of your old team be joining you soon?

No. I'm very happy with the personnel I've got here.

[*wages are normally given per week in the British game., e.g. 40,000 pounds **a week**]

1. The amount of money that a manager can spend on new players... : *transfer budget*
2. To improve the club's group of players... : _____
3. A player that a manager would like to sign... : _____
4. The amount of money which a potential new player wants to be paid if he joins the club... : _____
5. To get a new player without paying a transfer fee (because the player's contract at his current club has run out)... : _____
6. An agreement that a player will stay at the club for a longer period of time than first agreed... : _____
7. The personnel that help the manager to do his job (e.g. coaches, fitness coaches etc)... : _____

Ex. 3 These are extracts from newspaper reports. Can you guess what the words & phrases **in bold** mean?:

...City will **unveil** their new signing Vincent Lewis later today...
...Albion have **unveil**ed their new manager Philip Morgan...
...Bill Griffin has agreed a three-year deal with United and will be **unveil**ed as their new boss on Wednesday morning...

...Rumours are surfacing that players have lost faith in the manager and that he **lost the dressing room** long ago...
...the manager has **lost the dressing room** and the players are no longer backing him....
...sources close to key players report that the manager has **lost the dressing room**. Players are starting to ignore him and effectively refuse to play for him...

...the manager admitted that it would take the team **time to gel** after big changes to the squad during the summer...
...he recruited eight new players in the transfer window and they will require **time to gel**...
...maybe they simply need **time to gel** because so many new players have come in to freshen up an ageing squad...

...Hickman has been **linked with** a move to Wanderers as he considers leaving United...
...Albion, United and City have all been **linked with** a transfer move for the twenty-year-old forward...
...Steve Ayers has been **linked with** the England manager post as his contract with Rovers expires in the summer...

...The chairman assured fans that "success is essential" when questioned about the team's poor season so far, which will not be interpreted as **a vote of confidence** in the manager...
...Peter Campbell received **a vote of confidence** from the club's chairman yesterday after Wanderers' disappointing league campaign...
... the manager's sacking is just days after he was given **a vote of confidence** by the board following their 5-0 thrashing by Albion...

Ex. 4 Match the sentence halves. Then match the definitions to the words & phrases **in bold**:

1. The club are confident that he will **sign a new**... B/iv
2. All the players call the manager...
3. Rovers have appointed a new **director**...
4. Harry Stone will be the **caretaker**...
5. The clubs have agreed a transfer fee and the player is now negotiating his **personal**...

A. ...**gaffer**.
B. ...**deal** and put an end to the transfer rumours.
C. ...**of football**.
D. ...**terms** with United.
E. ...**manager** until a permanent appointment is made.

i. A common informal nickname for a manger. Used by players to talk about their manager.
ii. The parts of a player's contract which deal with his wages and sponsorship deals etc.
iii. The person who becomes the manager for a short period of time because the manager has been fired and the club are looking for a new manager.
iv. To agree a new contract.
v. A senior member of staff. He helps communication between the coach and the board of directors. He has more responsibility for the business side of operations than the coach, e.g. signing new players and negotiating contracts.

13. CHANCES

Ex. 1 If a player tries to score, but is unsuccessful, then we can call this an 'effort'. An effort means 'a try'. Put the words below in a logical order according to how good the effort was:

~~good~~ great decent fine poor

	1.		
	2.		
"That was a	3.	**effort**	by Smith!"
	4.	*good*	
	5.		

Ex. 2 If a player has a chance to score, we often want to say how easy or difficult it is. Put the words below in a logical order according to how difficult the chance was:

~~difficult~~ ~~easy~~ clear half simple decent

	1.	*easy*
	2.	
"That was a(n)	3.	**chance...."**
	4.	
	5.	*difficut*
	6.	

Ex. 3 This is an extract from a match report. Find the synonyms for the phrases below:

"…Wilkinson **got** 3 glorious **chance**s to score in the first half, but was unable to take any of them. On each occasion he was unlucky not to score, and was denied by some excellent defending and goalkeeping — the third of his efforts producing a fine save from Bailey. But after the break, his luck turned. Rovers continued to create chance after chance and when he found himself free in front of goal on 68 minutes, this time he didn't miss…"

1. to have a chance = to _get_ a chance.
2. to score = to _____ a chance.
3. to be unfortunate = to be _____.
4. to make a chance = to _____ a chance.
5. to have NO defender near you = to _____ yourself free.
6. to NOT score = to _____ a chance.

Ex. 4 When commentators give the reason why a player misses a chance, they often say he was 'denied by' something. Rearrange the mixed-up words below to complete the sentences:
(Example: 1= 'post')

*"Wilkinson produced a fine effort, only to be **denied by**…*

1. …the **stpo**." (the ball hit the side of the goal)
2. …the **ssrocarb**." (the ball hit the top of the goal)
3. …a fine **aves**."(the goalkeeper stopped the ball)
4. …a sliding **ckelta**."(a defender slid along the ground to take the ball)

Ex. 5 Match these sentence halves. They are things said by television commentators:

1. Wilkinson has had no luck **in front**... *C*

2. That was a great **long**...

3. Wilkinson was **clean**...

4. Wilkinson misses from **close**...

5. Wilkinson **went** very...

6. Wilkinson **shot** just...

7. Wilkinson **waste**s a...

A. ...**range**. *(he was near to the goal)*

B. ...**close**. *(he missed by a small amount)*

C. ...**of goal** today. *(he has been unlucky not the score)*

D. ...**wide**. *(his shot went to the side of the goal, missing by a small amount)*

E. ...**great opportunity** to put Rovers ahead. *(he missed a very good chance)*

F. ...**through on goal**. *(he only had the goalkeeper in front of him)*

G. ...**range effort** from Wilkinson. *(he shot from a long way)*

Ex. 6 These sentences are from match reports. Can you guess what the words & phrases **in bold** mean?

...Smith had been working hard for this chance all match but when it came he **squandered** it, blazing it wide with only the goalkeeper to beat...
...he will look back with regret on two **squandered** opportunities but otherwise he had a decent match...
...they **squandered** 3 good chances at the beginning of the second half, and it proved very costly...

...had Adams not **fluffed** his effort in front of an open goal in the first half to put his team 1-0 up, the result could have been very different...
...the midfielder had the best chance but **fluffed** his opportunity, totally missing the ball in the 8th minute...
...Cole **fluffed** a tap-in from two yards...

...they did a lot of attacking but chances were **few and far between**...
...chances were **few and far between** in the second half, but the best of them went to City...
...United were happy to sit back and wait for a chance to counter-attack. Unfortunately those chances were **few and far between**...

...their coach became more and more frustrated as attacks broke down and chances **went begging**...
...Harrison missed a penalty and dozens of other opportunities **went begging**...
...another chance **went begging** for Rovers — Graham watching the ball fly over from a free header six yards out...

...a fantastic pass from Jacobs put Meadows **one on one** with the City goalkeeper midway through the second half...
...his first goal was set up by a ball from Noble which sent him through for a **one on one** with Rogers...
...whenever he gets **one on one** with the keeper, you just know he'll score...

...he **miss**ed a **sitter** on 35 minutes, going for power and blasting it over from 8 yards out...
...Harris **miss**ed a **sitter** when presented with an easy chance...
...he **miss**ed a **sitter** against Rovers last week but the manager put his trust in him again for this match...

14. Form

Ex. 1 This is part of a preview of Rovers' next match (previews give the reader information about a match that will be played soon). Find the words & phrases which are defined below:

"...Rovers' form of late has been **inconsistent**. Some impressive results against the top sides have been contrasted with losses against bottom of the table strugglers. It is poor **away form** which is their biggest concern. They have only managed to win one of their last eight on their travels, and have now lost four away games in a row. The manager points to good **performances** in recent matches, but these need to be converted into **results** soon if Rovers are to avoid being sucked into a relegation fight. With a trip to **in-form** United this Saturday, it looks like they are unlikely to come away with any points..."

1. How well or badly a team has played in recent matches which are not at their home stadium, is the team's... : _away form_
2. If a team has played well in its recent matches then it is... : _____
3. A team cannot perform at the same level every match. They play very well and beat a top team, but then in the next match lose to a team they should beat. We can say they are... : _____
4. If a team wins or gets a draw then it gets a... : _____
5. If a team plays well (but maybe they don't win or get a draw) it is a good... : _____

Ex. 2 This is an extract from a match report. Fill in the gaps (*Ex.1* above will help you):

A. performances   D. row
B. home   E. consistent
C. ~~in~~   F. results

"...Wanderers' recent form has been very [1]_____, winning **four in a** [2]_____ and only **losing one**[3] _in_ **their last nine**. While [4]_____ haven't always been good, they are managing to **get** the [5]_____ and come away with the points. If they can continue their **fine** [6]_____ **form**, as well as their solid away form, promotion this season would definitely not be out of the question..."

Difficulty level 2: "Good to Know"
Ex. 3 Match the words and phrases with their definitions:

1. To be in form **E**
2. Relegation form
3. Promotion form
4. Championship-winning form
5. A good run of form

A. Good form. The team has got good results in all their recent matches.
B. Bad form. If this form continues the team will go down to the division below next season.
C. Very good form. If this form continues the team will win their division this season.
D. Good form. If this form continues the team will go up to the division above next season.
E. The team's form is good.

Ex. 4 Fill the gaps in these sentences:

A. at	D. their
B. home	E. in
C. ~~of~~	F. all

1. United are on an unbeaten run _of_ 6 games.
2. Rovers are unbeaten _____ six games.
3. Wanderers are unbeaten _____ home this season.
4. United have an unbeaten _____ record this season. (They haven't lost at their own stadium this season)
5. Rovers are unbeaten in _____ last 7.
6. Wanderers are unbeaten in _____ competitions. (They haven't lost any of their league or cup matches this season)

Ex. 5 These words often combine with 'form'. Put them in a logical order according to how good the form is:

A. impressive	D. top
B. fine	E. decent
C. ~~poor~~	

	1.	*poor*	
	2.		
"Smith is in	3.	**form**	at the moment."
	4.		
	5.		

15. STATISTICS

Difficulty level 1: "The Basics"
Ex. 1 Look at the match statistics in this table. Are these statements **true or false**?

	Team A	Team B
Goals scored	3	0
Possession (%)	48	52
Corners	6	5
Offsides	5	2
Fouls committed	8	10
Red cards	0	0
Yellow cards	2	3
Attempts on target	5	5
Attempts off target	9	2

1. Team B had a player sent off. *false*
2. Team B gave away more free kicks than Team A.
3. The winning team had control of the ball for longer than the losing team.
4. The referee booked a total of 5 players.
5. Team A shot or headed at Team B's goal 14 times.

Difficulty level 1: "The Basics"
Ex. 2 This is a table of a player's statistics for a single match. Are these statements **true or false**?

Goals	0	Passing accuracy (%)	92
Shots	2	Key passes	7
Assists	2	Tackles	9
Passes	64	Interceptions	2

1. He didn't score and didn't shoot. *false*
2. Two of his passes or crosses allowed a player on his team to score a goal.
3. His passes where unsuccessful nine percent of the time.
4. He stopped an opponent's pass (and then got the ball for himself) three times.
5. His passes allowed a player to shoot seven times.

16. Team Selection

Difficulty level 1: "The Basics"
Ex. 1 Some fans are talking about which players they think will play in their team's next match. Match their comments with the explanations:

1. "Thompson deserves **a place in the team**!" *C*
2. "Thompson will **be on the bench**."
3. "The manager will **rotate** the team."
4. "The manager will **pick a full-strength side**."
5. "Daniels will **be dropped**."

A. Some players who played in the last match will not play. Not because they did not play well, but because the manager wants to give them a rest, and wants to give other players the chance to play.

B. He will not play at the start of the match, but could be a substitute. He will not play because the manager thinks he did not play well in the last match.

C. He has not been in the team in the last few matches, but he should be. He has probably played well when he has come on as a substitute.

D. He will not play at the start of the game, but will be a substitute.

E. The best possible team will play.

Difficulty level 1: "The Basics"

Ex. 2 (The answers to *Ex.1* will help with this exercise.) This is an interview with a manager after a match. Fill the gaps:

A. rotation
B. rotate
C. place
D. ~~bench~~

E. dropped
F. drop
G. full-strength

You decided to rest some players today. Was that perhaps a bit risky?

No, we've got a strong squad*, and it's important that we [1]_____ , to give some players a break, and to make sure that everyone in the squad gets a chance to play, so they stay sharp.

*And Daniels only **made the** [2] bench **today** . Did you [3] _____ **him** after his recent poor performances?*

I think Daniels will be the first to admit that his form hasn't been the best of late. But, as I said, we have a [4]_____ **policy** to make sure that the whole squad stays sharp. Today it was Morris' turn and Thompson had a rest. That's all.

*Next week is a very important match for you. Will you **pick a** [5] _____ **side** for that, or will you continue with your rotation policy?*

Well, all our matches are important! They're all worth three points! We'll see how the squad trains this week and make a decision. But we've got a strong squad, and I don't have a fixed 'full-strength side' in my mind, it will change from week-to-week. It depends on who needs a rest, who's trained well etc.

*And will Thompson **get his** [6] _____ **back** in the team?*

Well he wasn't [7] _____ . We decided to give him a rest today. And, as I said, we'll make a decision about next week's team next week!

*[The squad is all the players who play for the football club and can be chosen to play in the team.]

Ex. 3 Match the sentence halves. Then match the phrases **in bold** to its explanation:

1. Underhill is **making his first**... *C/iii*
2. It's a very strong **starting**...
3. Matthews has played 3 games in 8 days and is **being**...
4. Johnson is **unavailable**...
5. Smith is injured, so Anderson will be...
6. It's a very **attacking line**...

A. ...**line up** from Rovers today.
B. ...**for selection** today.
C. ...**start** of the season today.
D. ...**up** from Rovers today.
E. ...**rested** today.
F. ...**skipper** for the day.

i. He isn't playing because the manager wants to give the player a break.
ii. He isn't playing because he can't play. Maybe he is injured, ill or is serving a suspension.
iii. He is in the team from the *beginning* of the match for the first time this season.
iv. The eleven players who begin the match.
v. He's captain.
vi. The team is designed to score goals rather than defend.

Ex. 4 (This exercise is the same type as *Ex.3*) Match the sentence halves. Then match the phrases **in bold** to its explanation:

1. The manager has opted to start Jones on the bench and bring him on as an...
2. It shows Wanderers' **strength in**...
3. Rovers are **fielding**...
4. The manager will be missing some...
5. Chambers is **making his**...
6. Hall **is a doubt**...

A. ...**debut** for Rovers today.
B. ...**impact player** if they are looking for a goal in the second half.
C. ...**regular**s due to injury today.
D. ...**for** Sunday after the knee injury he picked up in the defeat to United last week.
E. ...**a full-strength side** today.
F. ...**depth** when they have three twenty-million-pound players on the bench.

i. The best possible team is playing.
ii. A player who normally plays if he is fit.
iii. Perhaps he won't be able to play because of injury.
iv. The squad is very strong; if some players can't play, their replacements are very good.
v. He is a substitute who can be very effective in the last part of the match. Perhaps he is very quick and will be effective when the other players are tired.
vi. He is playing for the club for the first time.

17. The World Cup

Ex. 1 Match these word combinations, and then match them to the correct definition:

1. World *C/iv*
2. Extra
3. Group
4. Knockout
5. Penalty
6. World Cup

A. time
B. stages (x2)
C. champions
D. shootout
E. qualifier

i. The part of the tournament where 4 teams play against each other in a 'mini-league'.
ii. The part of the tournament where the loser of a match has to leave the tournament.
iii. The period of time over 90 minutes if a game ends with the scores level.
iv. The winner of the World Cup is called this.
v. This is what happens if the scores are level after 120 minutes.
vi. A match played before the World Cup to help decide which teams can go to the World Cup.

Ex. 2 Put these stages of the World Cup in the right order:

The second round
The semi-finals
The group stages *1*

The final
The quarter-finals

Ex. 3 This newspaper article is about England's chances at the World Cup. Find the words & phrases which are defined below:

We've got the stars, but what about the constellation?

With the **opening ceremony** this Sunday, everyone's talking about the World Cup. So just how well can our national team do this time round? England definitely have some world-class players in their 23-man squad, but there are doubts whether these stars can combine together to produce a world-class team. A FIFA ranking of number five in the world would seem to be somewhat flattering given a history of England qualifying relatively easily but then disappointing at the finals themselves. Most pundits expect England to advance to the knockout stages of the tournament as group win-

ners, given the relatively weak opposition in their group—and anything less could lead to an early exit as the runners-up will probably go on to meet the favourites Germany in the second round. And this is where England have traditionally faltered; when they draw top-class opposition in the knockout stages. While teams like Germany possess the tactical flexibility and discipline to prosper at this level, England will be relying on inspiring individual performances from stars like their Golden Boot tipped striker Whitley. So when the players line up for the national anthems at their opening match on Wednesday England fans will be hoping that history doesn't repeat itself, and that their stars can be part of a winning constellation.

1. The first 'event' of the tournament.... : _opening ceremony_
2. The group of players from which the team can be chosen... : _____
3. The official position in a list which rates how good international teams are... : _____
4. To go through to the part of the tournament after the group stages... : _____
5. The team that finishes in first place in their 'mini-league'... : _____
6. The team that finishes in *second* place in their 'mini-league'... : _____
7. The award given to the player who scores the most goals at the World Cup... : _____
8. The 'song' which is played for each country before an international match... : _____

Ex. 4 Below are definitions of words and example sentences.
Unscramble the words that are being defined:
(Example: 1='draw')

1. The event where the teams are put into their groups
   for the group stages:
   *"The **adrw** for the World Cup finals will be held in
   Barcelona on Saturday."*

2. A friendly match used as preparation:
   *"Germany will play a final **wamr up mgea** against Poland
   on Friday."*

3. The number of times a player has played for their
   national team:
   *"Smith has a record 117 **psca** for his country."*

4. The players and staff of a team at the World Cup:
   *"There is a good spirit in the Brazil **amcp**."*

5. The buildings, pitches and equipment etc. that a team
   uses to train:
   *"France's **training ilitiesfac** are located right next to
   their hotel."*

6. To attempt to become the hosts of a future World Cup:
   *"Spain has announced they will **bdi** for the 2022
   World Cup."*

7. To be given a special status which means a highly
   ranked team won't have to play against other highly
   ranked teams at the group stages:
   *"Portugal will be **sdedee** at the World Cup draw."*

18. The League

Difficulty level 1: "The Basics"
Ex. 1 Match the explanations with the words & phrases:

1. A competition where a group of teams play against each other over a season is called... : _a league_ G
2. The group of teams which a team has to play in a season is called... : _____
3. When a team wins a match in the league it gets... : _____
4. We can see how many points a team has by looking at... : _____
5. At the end of the season, the team with the least number of points in their division... : _____
6. At the end of the season, the team with the most number of points in their division... : _____
7. The team which has the second highest number of points usually... : _____
8. In some divisions, the teams which finish near the top of the division, but which do not get promoted automatically, play a mini-competition. The winner of this competition gets promoted. This competition is called... : _____

A. gets relegated
B. a division
C. the play-offs
D. the (league) table

E. points
F. gets promoted (, too)
G. a league
H. gets promoted

Ex. 2 Fill the gaps in these sentences. The answers to *Ex.1* will help you:

A.	won	D.	went
B.	relegation	E.	promotion
C.	~~top~~	F.	bottom

1. City are __*top*__ of the league. *(They're in first place)*
2. City have _____ the league. *(They're champions)*
3. City have got _____. *(They've been promoted)*
4. City are _____ of the league. *(They're in last place)*
5. City avoided _____. *(They managed to stay in the division)*
6. City _____ down. *(They got relegated)*

Ex 3. Two fans are discussing their team's chances for the coming season. At the end of last season their team was promoted. Fill the gaps (the answers to *Ex.1* & *Ex.2* will help you):

FAN A: We [1] __*g ot*__ **promotion** last season, which is great, but I think we were a bit lucky. Staying in this division will be really difficult. I'm not looking forward to getting beaten every week.

FAN B: I don't know... I don't think there's such a big difference in quality. We've invested in some good players in the summer. I think we'll definitely be able to **avoid** [2] **rel**_____. Maybe even [3] **g**_____ **into the play-off places**!

A: No chance! **The play** [4] _____! There are a lot of teams with lots of money to spend in this division. Promotion is out of the question, if you ask me.

B: Look at Wanderers. They [5] **fin**_____ **in the play-offs** last year. They didn't spend much money at all.

A: OK, but that doesn't happen very often. If we finish anywhere **above the relegation** [6] **pl**_____, I'll be very happy.

B: Me too. Above the relegation places **on** [7] **go**____ **difference**. That would suit me! But we can dream, can't we?

Ex. 4 Look at the league table below. Are these sentences **true or false**?

	Team	Pld	W	D	L	F	A	Diff	Pts
1	Hillford Rovers	6	5	1	0	22	5	17	16
2	Sommerhill City	6	5	1	0	19	5	14	16
3	Redford Wanderers	6	4	1	1	12	7	5	13
4	Medston Town	6	3	3	0	7	3	4	12
5	Portborough	6	3	2	1	6	2	4	11
17	Leighmouth United	6	0	4	2	4	7	-3	4
18	Bridgeforth Athletic	6	1	1	4	8	13	-5	4
19	Widcastle	6	1	1	4	3	8	-5	4
20	Fenbury Rangers	6	1	0	5	8	16	-8	3

Pld played   **W** won   **D** drawn   **L** lost   **F** goals scored ('for')   **A** goals scored against the team   **Diff** goal difference (F minus A)   **Pts** points

1. Hillford are **the leaders**. *true*
2. Medston are **in fourth position**.
3. Sommerhill and Redford are **level on points**.
4. Leighmouth are **in seventeenth place**.
5. Hillford are **three points clear**.
6. Hillford are **top of the league**.
7. Bridgeforth **have a goal difference of minus five**.
8. Fenbury are **bottom of the league**.
9. Medston are **in the play-off places**.
10. Leighmouth are **in the relegation zone**.
11. Bridgeforth are **in the relegation zone**.
12. Medston are **five points behind the leaders**.
13. Hillford and Sommerhill **are level on points**.
14. Sommerhill are **three points clear of Redford**.
15. Leighmouth are **in the play-off places**.
16. Redston and Medford are **level on points**.
17. Leighmouth are **above the relegation zone on goal difference**.
18. Hillford **are leading on goal difference**.
19. Medston are **nine points clear of the relegation zone**.
20. Fenbury are **two points from safety**.
21. Leighmouth are **in the bottom three**.
22. Redford are **in a play-off spot**.

Ex. 5 This is part of a report on the weekend's football action. There is only about a month before the end of the season. Find the words & phrases described below:

"...It's going to be an exciting **run in** this season, with the championship very much undecided, play-off places still up for grabs and six or seven teams fighting against relegation. Hillford Rovers stay top despite dropping points at home, only managing a draw against mid-table Grinsted United, which means Redford close the gap to only one point on the league-leaders after their convincing three-nil away win at Portborough. Portborough remain in the play-off places but fall to fifth position, and their recent poor form puts them in danger of missing out altogether. At the bottom, Flatsey move up three places, and climb out of the relegation zone thanks to a hard-fought two-one win at home to fellow relegation battlers Fenbury. Fenbury stay second from bottom but will have the chance to move out of the drop zone when they visit Bridgeford next week; three points there would see them clear on goal difference with a game in hand..."

1. The games near the end of the season are called... _the run in_
2. If a team is still the league leader we can say they... : _____
3. If a team doesn't get a win when they play at their own stadium we can say they... : _____
4. If a team has no chance of winning the league but is not at risk of relegation we can say they are... : _____
5. If a team gets more points than the team above them this week, we can say that they have... : _____
6. If a team's position improves by three places we can say that they... : _____
7. A synonym for 'the relegation places'... : _____
8. If a team has played one game less than another team then they have... : _____

19. FOOTBALL GROUNDS & THE PITCH

FOOTBALL GROUND: a synonym for football stadium.

Difficulty level 1: "The Basics"
Ex. 1 These are things said by some away fans outside the ground before a match. Find the words & phrases which are defined below (one per sentence):

"We're sitting in the South Stand."

"There are two huge new **video screen**s this season."

"I'll meet you at the turnstiles if we get lost, OK?"

"It's an all-seater stadium, so the stewards will tell you to sit down."

"Last time I was here was with work. We had a great view from one of the executive boxes."

"Don't get lost after the match. If we're late back for the coach, they'll leave without us!"

1. The big television on which you can watch replays of the action... : _video screen_
2. A part of a football stadium. Usually there are four of these. One at each end, and one on each side... : _____
3. The turning gate you go through to enter the ground... : _____
4. Parts of the stadium where you can watch the match in luxury. They are normally used by business people to entertain their clients etc... : _____
5. A road vehicle used to transport groups of people between cities... : _____
6. The members of staff who help you find your seat and are responsible for safety... : _____

Ex. 2 Match the words & phrases to the labels on the picture below:

1. The half-way line E
2. The goal line
3. The touchline
4. The byline
5. The penalty spot
6. A corner flag
7. The dugout
8. An advertising hoarding
9. The penalty box
10. The technical area
11. The six-yard box
12. The centre circle

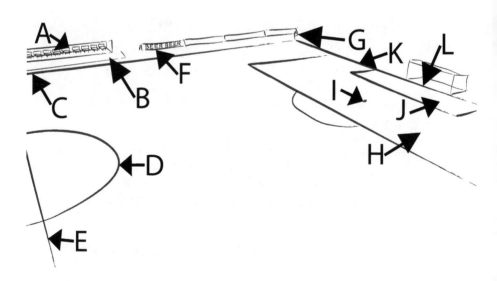

Ex. 3 These are things said by a TV football commentator. Use the definitions below to help you fill the gaps:

Astroturf: synthetic (plastic) grass.
Attendance: the number of people who are watching a match in the stadium.
CCTV: (closed-circuit television) a security camera system.
Capacity: the maximum number of people who can fit inside a football stadium.
Dressing room: the room in the stadium where players change into their kit before a match.
End: the part of the stadium behind a goal.

Floodlights: the high-powered lights used in stadiums to light up the pitch.
Terracing: an area of a stadium where people stand instead of sit.
Tier: one level of a football stadium. If a stadium has two tiers then seats right next to the pitch will be in the lower tier and the seats on the level above will be in the upper tier.
Tunnel: the entrance to the pitch for the players.
Undersoil heating: a system which prevents the pitch from freezing.

"The manager will surely have lots to say to the players in the [1]_dressing room_ at half-time."

"City plan to increase the [2]_____ of the stadium by adding a new [3]_____ of seating to the West Stand."

"The home team make their way slowly down the [4]_____ after a disappointing first-half."

"Today's official [5]_____ is fifty-nine thousand, four hundred and twenty-two."

"The away supporters in the north [6]_____ cheer the goalkeeper's mistake."

20. Mistakes

Difficulty level 1: "The Basics"
Ex. 1 These sentences are all from a television commentary. Match each sentence with an explanation:

1. "Johnson **gives the ball away** in a dangerous position." *C*

2. "Brown **miscontrol**s the ball and it goes out for a throw-in."

3. "Evans **lose**s **possession** in midfield."

4. "Davis **overhit**s that one and the goalkeeper collects."

5. "Wright **slip**s, but luckily Wilson is there to help out."

6. "Wood is **caught out of position** and can't get back in time."

A. He falls over because his foot slides on the ground.

B. He kicks the ball too hard when he is passing it.

C. He lets the other team get the ball. *(x2)*

D. He is not in the correct area of the pitch when the other team are attacking.

E. He doesn't control the ball successfully when he gets a pass or is dribbling with the ball.

Ex. 2 This is an extract from a match report of a match between United & Albion. Find the words and phrases **in bold** which are explained below:

"...Mistakes cost United dearly in the second half. First, the defence **switch**ed **off** and allowed Roberts acres of space in the box to convert Clark's speculative cross to make it one-nil. Then it was further **lapse**s **of concentration** which led to the second goal six minutes later. Thomas was **caught in possession** on the half-way line, Albion countered swiftly, which was temporarily broken up by a great interception by Wilson, only for him to immediately lose possession again with **a misplaced pass**. Walker gratefully received the ball on the edge of the box and rifled a shot low and hard into the bottom-right corner. And to complete a hat trick of gifts for Albion, Lewis was easily **dispossessed** by Roberts deep into the United half with three minutes left on the clock. Walker was free at the far post and Roberts found him with a perfect cross to which he applied a simple headed finish..."

1. An inaccurate pass... :   *a misplaced pass*

2. To have the ball taken off you by an opponent *(x2)*... :   _____   _____

3. When you lose concentration for a short time *(x2)*... :   _____   _____

Ex. 3 These sentences are all from match reports. Can you guess what the words & phrases **in bold** mean?

...a fantastic dribble was spoilt by the finish; wildly **blast**ing **over** the bar from the right-hand edge of the box...
...Brown set up the shot perfectly only for Evans to **blast over**...
...the striker rushed the chance and wastefully **blasted over**...

...White took advantage of another **defensive blunder** inside the box to score his thirtieth goal of the season...
... a minute after half-time a **defensive blunder** gifted Albion the lead...
...A **defensive blunder** by Jones five minutes into the second half presented Taylor with a fantastic chance to bring the scores level...

...Stewart dropped another **clanger**, leaving Martin free to score easily from close range...
...a defensive **clanger** cost City two points at Rovers last week...
...the centre-back definitely has talent, but also the habit of dropping the occasional **clanger**. His one today was horrendous...

...Wanderers were **undone** by two goals in the space of ten minutes...
...the home team attacked in search of a second only to be **undone** when Jackson rose above James to head in minutes before the final whistle...
...Davis' side were **undone** by a series of defensive errors...

21. Training

Difficulty level 1: "The Basics"
Ex. 1 Read these things a coach says to his players. Then match the words & phrases **in bold** to the pictures:

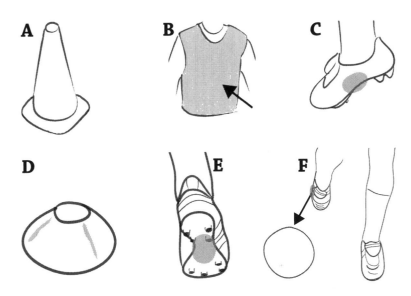

A   B   C

D   E   F

1. "...then pass it with the **outside of the boot** to the next player..." *picture F*

2. "...then pass it with the **the instep** to the next player..."

3. "...roll the ball backwards with the **sole of the foot**..."

4. ...dribble to the **cone** and then pass to the player on the other side..."

5. "...take two **marker**s and make a small goal..."

6. "...everyone on this team put on a **bib**..."

Ex. 2 Read this text of a coach explaining his plans to his players. Find the words & phrases which are defined below:

"...OK, in this **session** we're mainly going to be working on defending. So we'll be doing some **drills** to practise defending crosses. We'll finish up with some **five-a-sides**, but to start with let's do our warm up **stretches**, followed by some jogging and then **sprints**..."

1. One period of training... : _a session_
2. Short, quick runs... : _____
3. An exercise, repeated many times, to train a particular skill... : _____
4. A practice game of football with a small number of players on each team... : _____
5. Physical exercises to prepare the body (e.g. muscles) for doing sport... : _____

Ex. 3 Complete this sentence with the options in the two lists below:
*(Example: 1=G ...work on **passing & moving**)*

"In this drill we're going to work on...

1. ...passing...
2. ...creating...
3. ...ball...
4. ...accurate...
5. ...set...
6. ...retaining...
7. ...making...

A. ...passing." *(kicking the ball to another player on your team very exactly)*

B. ...yourself available." *(running into the best areas of the pitch so that it is easy for teammates to pass to you)*

C. ...space." *(using the whole area of the pitch so there is more room to attack)*

D. ...pieces." *(corners, free kicks and throw-ins)*

E. ...control." *(the ability to move the ball around very exactly when it is close to you)*

F. ...possession." *(keeping the ball)*

G. ... and moving." *(giving the ball to another player and then running into space so you can receive the ball again or make defenders come to you instead of to the player on the ball)*

Ex. 4 Read these things which a coach says to his players at a training session. Match the words & phrases **in bold** to the definitions below:

1. "Right, now twenty minutes of **two-touch** five-a-side." *C*
2. "Right let's **cool down** before we go back to the changing rooms."
3. "OK, get into groups of three and practice **keep-ups**. Four keep-ups, then with your fifth touch pass it, in the air, to the next person."
4. "Everyone gather around the **chalkboard** and we'll have a look at what went wrong with our defending on Saturday."
5. "The object of this exercise is to improve our **awareness**."
6. "OK, remember, in this drill, I want to see a good **body shape** and your [7.] **plant foot** in the right position."
8. "Our **movement** wasn't good on Saturday so we need to work on that today."

A. The skill of kicking the ball many times without letting it touch the ground.
B. How well members of a team run into different spaces and positions (in order to create passing opportunities and to make it harder for the other team to defend).
C. Describes a 'rule' for a game or drill which means the players are only allowed to make contact with the ball twice before possession has to go to another player.
D. A black writing surface on which a coach can draw tactical diagrams.
E. The physical position of a player's arms, legs, head etc. when he kicks or gets the ball, e.g. if a player has his head up or down, or his shoulders open or closed.
F. The foot which is *not* going to kick the ball.
G. The ability to know the location of other players and the directions in which they are moving, even though you cannot always see these players.
H. The opposite of 'warm up'.

22. Calls

Ex. 1 These are some common calls that you will hear on a football pitch. Match each one to the description of its function below:

1. "Turn!" *D*
2. "Play on!"
3. "Push out!" / "Push up!"
4. "Man on!"

5. "Time!"
6. "To feet!"
7. "Switch it!"
8. "Square!"

9. "Mark up!"
10. "Far post!"
11. "Jockey him!"
12. "Down the line!"

A. An instruction to pass the ball along the side of the pitch. Often a long ball in the air.

B. An instruction by the referee that play should continue (e.g. when some players think a foul has been committed, but the referee disagrees).

C. An instruction to pass the ball 90° left of right (rather than forward or backwards).

D. An instruction to a player who has control of the ball that he has enough time to turn 180° with the ball.

E. Information for the player who has the ball that he does not have to rush because no opponent is nearby.

F. An instruction that the defensive line should move up the pitch together (e.g. when the ball has been successfully cleared away from the goal after a corner).

G. A warning to a teammate that an opponent is nearby.

H. A request that you want to receive a pass directly to you along the ground (rather than a pass into space, and then running to get the ball, or a pass in the air).

I. An instruction to cross the ball towards the side of the goal which is furthest away from the ball.

J. An instruction to a defender who is trying to get the ball from an attacker on the other team that he should not take any risks, and just slow the player down, rather than trying to make a tackle.

K. An instruction to move the ball as quickly as possible to the opposite wing.

L. An instruction to the players on the defending side that they should choose a player on the other side, and stay close to this player, to prevent him getting the ball.

23. Injuries

Difficulty level 1: "The Basics"
Ex. 1 These are sentences from newspaper articles. Fill the gaps with this list of words:

A. unavailable   E. recovered
B. ~~for~~   F. back
C. bandage   G. have
D. physio   H. term

- White will be **out** [1] _for_ the rest of the season. *[White is injured and will not be able to play until next season]*

- Evans will [2] _____ **surgery on** his broken foot later this week. *[Evans will have an operation to help heal his injury]*

- Jenkins will be [3] _____ for Albion's trip to United on Saturday. *[Jenkins can't play in the next match, maybe because he is injured]*

- The [4] _____ ran on to the pitch. *[A player is injured and the member of staff responsible for treating injuries went to help him]*

- Green returned after half-time with a [5] _____ on his head. *[He got a head injury in the first-half. It is now protected with a piece of white cloth]*

- The manager announced that Wright has [6] _____ **from** his ankle injury and will be back for their next match. *[He is now fit again after being injured]*

- Wilson is due to come [7] _____ from a **long-** [8] _____ ankle injury next week. *[He will play next week after being injured for a long time]*

Ex. 2 Below is a list of common football injuries. Match them to their descriptions. Then match the letters on the picture:

These definitions will help you:
Ligament: the material inside the body which joins one bone to another bone.
Tendon: the material inside the body which connects muscle to bone.
Cartilage: the flexible material inside the body found where two bones join.

1. Torn cartilage *iv/A*
2. Sprained ankle
3. Hamstring strain
4. Groin strain

5. Cruciate ligament injury
6. A dead leg
7. A stress fracture

i. The ligaments which connect the bottom of the leg to the foot are damaged. Often when a player twists this part of the body unnaturally.

ii. One of the main ligaments in the knee is damaged. It can be a very serious injury.

iii. The muscles on the inside of the top of the leg are stretched too far and damaged.

iv. Normally a knee injury that happens when the knee cartilage is damaged because all of the player's weight is on one leg when he turns unnaturally.

v. A small crack in a bone, caused by high impact on it over a long period of time. Often happens to bones in the foot.

vi. A muscle that runs down the back of the leg is stretched too far and damaged.

vii. Muscles in the leg are torn when a player is hit powerfully by another player, e.g. by the other player's knee.

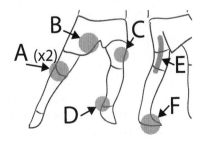

Ex. 3 Here are two extracts from newspaper articles. Find the words & phrases which are defined below each extract:

"...however there is better news regarding Jackson, who will be back in action much sooner than originally thought. The centre-back **was stretchered off** in Saturday's one-one draw with City after a collision with his own goalkeeper. Initial reports suggested he would be sidelined for six weeks, but the manager has confirmed that he's just picked up a knock and will be back in training tomorrow..."

1. To be carried from the pitch on a stretcher because the player cannot/should not walk... : *to be stretchered off*
2. An 'accident' caused by two players running into each other... : _____
3. To be unable to play because of injury... : _____
4. To get a minor injury... : _____

"...Wanderers' injury crisis has deepened after yesterday's match. Wood joins six other regular first-team starters on the treatment table, and the prognosis doesn't look good; a three to four week lay-off likely with a hamstring injury. Another of their hamstrung players Mason has suffered a setback and will not be able to return to training this week as first thought..."

5. A very difficult situation for a club caused because so many players are injured... : _____
6. A synonym phrase for 'injured'... : _____
7. A judgement by medical staff about how serious an injury is, and how long it will take to recover from this injury... : _____
8. An adjective meaning 'to have a hamstring injury'... : _____
9. To have a new problem which means it will take longer to recover from the injury than expected... : _____

24. FANS

Difficulty level 1: "The Basics"

Ex. 1 These are things said by fans during a match. Match the words **in bold** with the list of alternative words:

1. The away **supporters** have been very quiet since we scored! *B*
2. I don't know why I **support** this team sometimes!
3. The **crowd** isn't very loud today!
4. The away fans are **chant**ing a song about the manager.
5. I only need Charlie Coal and then I've completed my sticker **album**!

A. sing

B. fans *(x2)*

C. follow

D. book

Difficulty level 1: "The Basics"

Ex. 2 Match the words **in bold** with the list of definitions below:

1. I'm going to buy a **replica shirt** with Hall's name on the back, I think he's fantastic! *B*
2. I've got all of United's **programme**s for the last 20 years.
3. My daughter was a **mascot** at City last year.
4. There was an electric **atmosphere** at the match on Wednesday night.
5. Some fans threw a **flare** on the pitch and the match had to be stopped for five minutes.
6. There were lots of **banner**s in the crowd asking for a new manager.

A. A child who comes on to the pitch with the captain of a team before a match.
B. A shirt that looks exactly like the ones that the players wear when they are playing.
C. A firework often used by fans. It burns very brightly for a short time and creates a lot of smoke.
D. A big piece of material or paper with a message written on it that fans hold up in the stadium.
E. The thin book sold by the home team at a match. It tells you the names of the players, the dates of other matches, contains articles and a message from the manager.
F. The feeling inside the stadium during a match.

Difficulty level 3: "Advanced"
Ex. 3 These are sentences from different newspaper articles. Find the words & phrases which are defined below in the sentences (one for each sentence):

1. ...police managed to stop a full-scale pitch invasion after about twenty fans managed to get on to the pitch at the final whistle...

2. ...a group of fans, who were protesting at the lack of investment in the team, ripped up their **season ticket**s and threw them at the manager...

3. ...Atkinson was booed off the pitch after another awful performance...

4. ...after Albion went three-nil up the crowd greeted every pass with a loud cheer...

5. ...the team were given a muted reception by the fans after their poor first-half performance...

6. ...Albion fans were buoyed this week after the announcement of the signing of two new attacking players...

A. A small book containing tickets for home matches for one year... : _a season ticket_

B. To welcome someone or something less enthusiastically than normal ... : _____

C. To make someone feel confident and hopeful... : _____

D. To make a noise which shows you do *not* like something... : _____

E. When hundreds of fans run on to the playing area during or after a match... : _____

F. A noise which shows you *do* like something... : _____

25. The Goal

Difficulty level 1: "The Basics"
Ex. 1 This is a list of parts of the goal. Match each item to a label on the picture:

1. The top-right corner *A*
2. The bottom-left corner
3. The post
4. The crossbar/the bar
5. The side-netting
6. The roof of the net

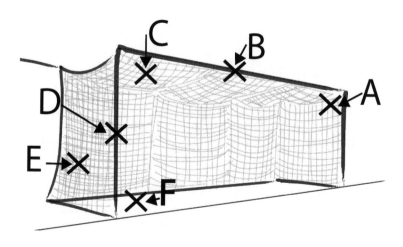

84

Ex. 2 Use these words to fill the gaps in the sentences from match reports below:

• over • off • rattled • woodwork • ~~post~~

"Walker's shot **struck the** [1]_post_ and Hall was first to the rebound to make it one-nil."

"The ball **came** [2]_____ **the post** safely into the keeper's hands."

"Peterson got up well for the header but could only direct it [3]_____ **the bar**."

"James [4]_____ **the crossbar** with a powerful drive."

"Wanderers were lucky and were **saved by the** [5]_____ three times."

Ex. 3 These are phrases from *Ex.2*. Match them to the definitions:

• ~~over the bar~~ • to come off the post • to rattle the crossbar
• to be saved by the woodwork • to strike the post

1. A shot which misses. It is too high... : _over the bar_
2. To hit the top part of the goal very hard... : _____
3. To be lucky because the ball hits the post or the crossbar, and doesn't go in the goal... : _____
4. To hit the post *(x2)*... : _____   _____

26. Fixtures

A Fixture: an official arrangement that one team will play against another team.

Difficulty level 2: "Good to Know"
Ex. 1 Read this extract from a Rovers fan's internet blog. Find the words & phrases which are defined below:

"...The premier league **fixture list** was released earlier today, and what immediately stands out is that Rovers will start and finish the season with derbies. On the opening day of the season we travel to Albion, and on the last day there's a trip to Wanderers to look forward to. But apart from that last match, our run in looks pretty good: out of the last seven matches, five are at home; and all seven of those matches are against teams who finished in the bottom half of the table last season. So the toughest part of this campaign will probably be around Christmas when we play all of last season's top four!..."

1. The official plan for when teams in a league will play against each other... : _fixture list_
2. Matches against teams that are geographically close to each other... : _____
3. A synonym for 'the first day of the season'... : _____
4. The last few league matches of the season... : _____
5. A synonym for 'season'... : _____

Ex. 2 Find the phrases which are defined below by matching words in the two lists:

1. A match which is not a normal league match, but part of a cup competition. *F/ii 'a cup tie'*
2. A match which starts earlier than normal.
3. The amount of tickets that are reserved for away supporters.
4. The second of the two matches when teams have to play each other home and away in a cup competition.
5. A match which is played on Tuesday, Wednesday or Thursday.
6. The time when no football matches are played.

A.	an early	i.	game
B.	a midweek	ii.	tie
C.	the close	iii.	allocation
D.	the ticket	iv.	leg
E.	the second	v.	kick off
F.	a cup	vi.	season

Ex. 3 Sometimes matches cannot be played and they are cancelled. We often say that a match has been '**called off**' or '**postponed**' when it has been cancelled. Often the reason a match is called off is the condition of the pitch. A referee will sometimes have to carry out a '**pitch inspection**' before the match to decide if the pitch is good enough to play on. Match these reasons for calling off a match with their explanations:

"Today's match has been called off due to…

1. …snow." **D**
2. …a frozen pitch."
3. …a waterlogged pitch."
4. …fog."

A. Thick cloud is at ground level which makes it difficult to see.
B. The playing surface is too hard because it is so cold.
C. The playing surface is too wet because it has rained so much.
D. Too much snow is on the pitch, which can't be cleared in time.

27. GOALKEEPING

Difficulty level 2: "Good to Know"
Ex. 1 Arrange these mixed up sentences (describing action involving the goalkeeper) into the correct order:

1. made great the keeper a save.
   The keeper made a great save
2. from save that was a the keeper fine.
3. with the keeper his saved feet.
4. the keeper away from danger the ball punched.
5. for the defender left it the keeper.

Difficulty level 2: "Good to Know"
Ex. 2 Match the descriptions of action with the situations:

1. That was an awful **goalkeeping error**! F
2. That was a great **stop**!
3. Hopkins was **denied by the keeper**!
4. The goalkeeper was **unsighted**.
5. The keeper managed to make a **finger-tip save**.
6. The keeper managed to **get a touch to it**.
7. The keeper needs to work on his **distribution**.

A. The goalkeeper made a very good save.
B. The keeper couldn't catch the ball but he could make contact with the ball (e.g. to stop a striker getting the ball).
C. The goalkeeper's view was blocked by players in front of him.
D. The goalkeeper stopped the striker scoring.
E. The keeper saved the ball with the end of his fingers.
F. The goalkeeper made a bad mistake.
G. The goalkeeper should improve how he throws and kicks the ball to the players on his team.

Ex. 3 Match the pairs of descriptions of the same situations. Then match the definition of the words & phrases **in bold:**

1. "That was poor **decision making** from the keeper." *F/ii*
2. "That was an absolute **howler** from the keeper."
3. "The keeper was **wrong-footed** there."
4. "The keeper just **flap**ped at it."
5. "The keeper **claim**ed the ball."
6. "The keeper could only **parry** it out to the oncoming striker."

A. "Instead of pushing it out he managed to turn it into his own net!"
B. "The keeper comes off his line and takes the ball safely into his hands."
C. "The keeper tried to get the ball but it was out of his reach."
D. "He saves but the ball drops to Evans who scores."
E. "The striker sent the keeper the wrong way with a clever drop of the shoulder."
F. "The keeper should have stayed on his line instead of coming out to try and get the ball."

i. To move or dive in one direction, but the ball is kicked in the other direction.
ii. The quality of the keeper's judgement when deciding when and where to move and run.
iii. A really bad mistake.
iv. To make a save by pushing the ball away from the goal.
v. To move towards the ball and catch it confidently.
vi. To wave your hand around in an unsuccessful attempt to get to the ball.

Ex. 4 Match the sentence halves. Then match the definition of the words & phrases **in bold:**

1. "The keeper dived to...
2. "What a spectacular **double**... E/ii
3. "That was poor...
4. "He was their **second**...
5. "It's not an easy job **between**...

A. ...**choice goalkeeper** last season."
B. ...**the sticks**."
C. ...**smoth**er the ball."
D. ...**positioning** from the keeper."
E. ...**save** from the keeper!"

i.   A team's number-two goalkeeper.
ii. To make a save and then immediately another save.
iii. To dive on top of the ball and cover it with your upper body.
iv. A synonym phrase for 'goalkeeping'.
v.   Where the keeper decides to stand when his goal is being attacked.

28. Heading

Difficulty level 1: "The Basics"
Ex. 1 Match these sentences to the explanations:

1. "Smith **head**ed it **in**." *B*
2. "Smith **head**ed it **over**."
3. "Smith **head**ed it **out**."
4. "Smith **head**ed it **away**."
5. "Smith **head**ed it **on**."

A. He tried to score but missed, it was too high.
B. He scored a goal.
C. He 'passed' the ball with his head; using the power already on the ball, but changing the ball's direction so it went to one of his teammates.
D. He was defending and headed the ball (probably powerfully) to a safer area, not near his goal.
E. He was defending and decided to head the ball behind the goal (for a corner), or over the touchline (for a throw-in).

Difficulty level 3: "Advanced"
Ex. 2 These words often combine with 'header'. Match them to the definitions below:

1. A **powerful** header. *C*
2. A **diving** header.
3. A **free** header.
4. A **looping** header.
5. A **glancing** header.

A. It is easy for the player to head the ball because he isn't challenged by a member of the opposition.
B. The player doesn't make much contact with the ball, changing the direction of the ball with only a small touch.
C. The ball is headed with a lot of force.
D. The player throws himself in the air towards the ball. His body is parallel to the ground when he heads the ball.
E. The ball goes high is the air, it flies in a 'curve' rather than directly to its target.

29. Timing

Difficulty level 1: "The Basics"

Ex. 1 These are things which fans said during a match. Replace the underlined words and phrases with more formal synonyms from the list (which, for instance, television commentators often use):

A. stoppage
B. remaining
C. the restart

D. period
E. ~~the interval~~

1. "There's only a couple of minutes until **half-time**." *E*
2. "There's only ten minutes **to go**. We need to score soon!"
3. "Look! There's going to be 5 minutes of **injury** time!"
4. "The team's not fit enough. They're going down with cramp in the **first half of extra time**!"
5. "We've looked much better since **half-time**."

Difficulty level 2: "Good to Know"

Ex. 2 These sentences are all from match reports. Replace the underlined words & phrases with their synonyms:

A. in the last couple of minutes
B. towards the end
C. at the beginning

D. ~~halfway~~
E. after the break

1. "United scored **midway through** the first half." *D*
2. "Rovers were nervous **during the opening minutes** of the match."
3. "Albion equalised ten minutes **into the second half**."
4. "Wanderers were by far the stronger team **during the closing stages**."
5. "Wilson got the winner in the **dying moments** of the match."

30. MISCELLANEOUS

Ex. 1 These are things said by fans. Match the sentence halves:

1. "I missed the match but I'll **watch** the... *B*
2. "We need to sign a new quality striker, we need someone **world**...
3. "A draw would be a good result because the...
4. "Hall is injured so I think the manager should **give** the **captain's**...
5. "Have you seen the new **away**...
6. "He scored a fantastic free kick. It must have been twenty...

A. ...**armband to** Wilson."
B. ...**highlights** tonight on television."
C. ...**kit**? The colour's awful!"
D. ...**yards** out."
E. ...**replay** would be at home."
F. ...**class**."

Ex. 2 Are these pairs of words & phrases the same or different?

1. a commentator / a presenter   *different*
2. soccer / football
3. the favourites / the underdogs
4. against / versus
5. The Football Association / The Premier League
6. trophies / silverware

Difficulty level 2: "Good to Know"
Ex. 3 These sentences are from match reports. Complete the missing prepositions in the phrases **in bold**:

A. down
B. from
C. on
D. behind

E. ~~in~~
F. against
G. out

1. ...Walker showed that he is most comfortable with the ball played up to him _in_ **the air**, and is excellent at knocking balls down for Roberts to run on to, or holding the ball up until the midfield can join the attack...

2. ...Athletic have transformed themselves into a team who like to play the ball _____ **the ground** and create chances with patient passing...

3. ...United set out to frustrate Wanderers and **put ten men** _____ **the ball** from the start...

4. ...Albion **went** _____ **to ten men** early in the second half when Evans received a red card for a reckless tackle...

5. ...The manager couldn't risk resting some of his key players ahead of Rovers' Champions League match on Tuesday and **put** _____ **a strong team** today...

6. ...City **are tied** _____ their local rivals United in the next round of the cup...

7. ...Wright scored a hat trick today despite announcing that he would **retire** _____ **the game** at the end of the season after a career of almost twenty years...

Ex. 4 These are things said by television football commentators. Fill the gaps and match the phrases **in bold** to their definitions:

A. winning D. strip

B. cup E. ~~outside~~

C. shin

1. "...most have given Rovers only an _outside_ **chance** of getting a result today..." *iii*

2. "...Albion are wearing their new **away** _____ for the first time this season. Traditionalists are not happy with the shade of blue chosen, saying it's far too dark..."

3. "...Green is unavailable for tonight's Champions League match because he **is** _____ **tied**, having already played in the Champions League group stages for United before his transfer in January..."

4. "...Wanderers need to show their famous _____ **mentality** today, as only three points will be good enough..."

5. "...The manager seems to be very annoyed with Jones as he wasn't ready to come on as substitute because he appears to have lost his _____ **pads**..."

i. A way of thinking which means beating the other team is the most important thing.

ii. The playing clothes that a team often wears when they are not playing at home.

iii. A small possibility.

iv. The protection which players wear to protect the front of their legs (below the knee).

v. To be unable to play in a particular competition because you have already played for another team in that competition earlier in the season.

Ex. 5 These are things said by television football commentators. Fill the gaps and match the words & phrases **in bold** to their definitions:

A. journeyman
B. grassroots
C. ~~loose~~

D. at
E. fixing
F. gamesmanship

1. "...Clarke picks up the _loose_ **ball** from the corner but shoots just wide..." *iii*
2. "...There **is a lot** _____ **stake** for Rovers today. A loss would make Champions League qualification almost impossible..."
3. "...The last time that these two teams met, police were asked to investigate **match** _____ allegations, but both teams were cleared of any wrong doing..."
4. "...Albion's _____ in the second half is starting to annoy the home fans and they are booing and whistling anything which they feel is time-wasting..."
5. "...The children who you can see playing on the pitch at half-time are all from local _____ **football** projects which are being sponsored by Rovers..."
6. "...The _____ striker Jackson will be looking for yet another club next season as it was announced that Wanderers aren't going to extend his contract for another season..."

i. Football played by amateurs in schools and small clubs.
ii. Play which is on the border of being against the rules, e.g. diving to try and get a penalty, pretending to be injured to waste time, standing on the ball when the other team has been awarded a free kick etc.
iii. A moment when the ball is not under the control of any player and so is 'free' for a player nearby to get. This usually happens because the ball has bounced randomly off a player's head or body, or off the post or crossbar, or maybe because the keeper has made a save but can't control where the ball goes afterwards.
iv. A player who has played for many different clubs and is not a star player.
v. When a team deliberately loses a match because it has been agreed in advance.
vi. Describing a situation where a lot can be lost if a team does not win.

ANSWER KEY

1 KICKING & MOVING THE BALL

Ex.1
1. B **5.** A **9.** H
2. J **6.** C **10.** G
3. D **7.** I
4. E **8.** F

Ex.2
1. back / D
2. crossed / B
3. touch / E
4. half-volley / C
5. long-ball / A

Ex.3
1. upfield
2. to flick (the ball **on to** another player)
3. a one-two
4. first-touch
5. a low cross
6. first-time
7. a chip (can also be used as a verb: 'to chip')

Ex.4
1. B **5.** F
2. H **6.** A
3. D **7.** C
4. E **8.** G

Ex.5
1. pinging
2. dinked
3. reverse pass
4. punts
5. knock-on
6. the inside-right channel

2 POSITIONS

Ex.1
1. J/K
2. E
3. G/H
4. A
5. F
6. C/D
7. B
8. I

Ex.2
1. C **5.** F **9.** J
2. H **6.** I **10.** G
3. K **7.** E **11.** B
4. D **8.** A

3 DESCRIBING A GAME

Ex.1
1. E **3.** F **5.** B
2. A **4.** C **6.** D

Ex.2
1. B - final (ten minutes)
2. E - early on
3. C - composed
4. A - lucky
5. D - impressive

Ex.3
1. B
2. F
3. G (to **give** credit to someone)
4. D
5. A
6. C
7. E (to **show** spirit)
8. H

Ex.4
1. E **4.** G **7.** C
2. H **5.** B **8.** D
3. A **6.** I **9.** F

Ex.5

1. A	**4.** E	**7.** G
2. F	**5.** B	**8.** D
3. H	**6.** C	**9.** I

4   ATTACKING

Ex.1

1. H	**4.** E	**7.** D
2. C	**5.** G	**8.** B
3. A	**6.** F	

Ex.2

1. A	**5.** D	**9.** H
2. F	**6.** C	**10.** K
3. E	**7.** J	**11.** I
4. B	**8.** G	

Ex.3

1. F	**4.** G	**7.** H
2. C	**5.** D	**8.** I
3. A	**6.** B	**9.** E

Ex.4

1. To chase the game: a team is chasing the game when they are behind (the other team has more goals) and they are attacking and taking risks in order to score.

2. To cut in (from the left/right): a player sharply changes the direction of his run. At first he is running down one of the wings, then he turns sharply towards the centre of the pitch.

3. To (be)/(to put a team) under siege: a team is under siege when the other team is attacking constantly for a long period. The team under siege find it difficult to get possession of the ball, and to build their own attacks.

4. To find an opening: to find a space in a defence. The ball can then be passed through this space to set up a shot on goal.

5   DEFENDING

Ex.1

1. C	**4.** B	**7.** F
2. E	**5.** D	
3. A	**6.** G	

Ex.2

1. unmarked
2. dragged out of position
3. make a challenge
4. close a player down
5. playing an offside-trap
6. playing a flat back-four
7. a sliding tackle
8. to cover

Ex.3

1. A	**4.** B	**7.** C
2. F	**5.** G	
3. D	**6.** E	

Ex.4

1. defending too high up
2. splits the defence
3. central-defensive partnership
4. tight (to the player)
5. defensive frailties
6. at the back
7. to shield the ball
8. (to be) goalside

Ex.5

1. B/ii (to make a goal-line clearance)
2. C/iii (to win the ball cleanly)
3. D/iv (a zonal marking system)
4. A/i (a solid defence)

Ex.6

1. D/i (pressing game)
2. E/v (two-footed lunge)
3. B/iv (all over the place)
4. C/iii (to pick someone up)
5. A/ii (defensive record)

Ex.7

1. D/iv (to commit too early)

2. B/i (to drop back into defence)

3. C/ii (to make a last-ditch tackle)

4. A/iii (to stem the tide)

6   TACTICS

Ex.1

1. D	**4.** F	**7.** C
2. A	**5.** B	
3. E	**6.** G	

Ex.2

1. (to) create space

2. (to) dominate possession

3. (to) put out a defensive side

4. closing down

5. (a) direct (style of play)

6. (a) free role

7. (to) switch the play

Ex.3

1. C

2. D

3. A (To track = to follow another player when he runs into attacking positions)

4. B

5. E

Ex.4

1. D	**3.** A
2. B	**4.** C

Ex.5

1. D

2. C (i.e. they had one more player compared to the other team)

3. F

4. A (retain the ball = keep possession of the ball)

5. B

6. E

Ex.6

1. D	**3.** F	**5.** A
2. C	**4.** B	**6.** E

7   THE RULES & THE REFEREE

Ex.1

1. B	**4.** D	**7.** E
2. F	**5.** A	
3. G	**6.** C	

Ex.2

1. C

2. E (A trip: a player makes another player fall by catching his foot or leg)

3. A

4. D

5. B (A dive: a player tries to trick the referee by falling over even though he hasn't been fouled)

6. F (Time-wasting: taking longer than necessary to do things like take throw-ins or corners, or pretending to be injured, because it is near the end of the match and your team is winning)

Ex.3

1. "The referee gave a free kick for handball." / D

2. "The referee blew the whistle for half-time." / A

3. "The referee booked him for a bad tackle." / C

4. "The referee sent him off for dangerous play." / E

5. "The referee played the advantage." / B

Ex.4

1. D/iv

2. A/ii

3. F/i

4. E/vi

5. B/iii

6. C/v

Ex.5

1. D	**2.** F	**3.** B

4. A **6.** E
5. G **7.** C

Ex.6
1. D **4.** F **7.** E
2. G **5.** A **8.** C
3. B **6.** H

Ex.7
1. (To be) **on a booking**: to already have one yellow card.
2. **A tug**: a short, sharp pull on something, e.g. on a player's shirt or arm.
3. **An infringement**: a foul, or something else which is against the rules.
4. To **penalise** someone: to 'punish' them for breaking the rules, e.g. by giving a free kick.
5. **A stonewall penalty**: a very, very clear penalty.
6. (To be) **ineligible** (to play): not having the necessary permission to play for a team or to play in a particular competition.

Ex.8
1. (to) point to the spot
2. a penalty appeal
3. a spot-kick
4. to clip someone
5. a soft penalty
6. a bookable offence
7. a penalty shout

8. an incident

8 THE SCORE & RESULTS

Ex.1
1. F (**to thrash a team**: to beat them by lots of goals)
2. C
3. D
4. E
5. B ('to draw' is an irregular verb; *draw, drew, have drawn*)
6. A

Ex.2
1. 'to come from behind'
2. 'to get a result'
3. 'at one-nil down'
4. 'to finish one-one'
5. 'to be behind'

Ex.3
1. upsets
2. rout
3. (shock) result
4. convincing (win)
5. registered (a win)

9 SCORING GOALS

Ex.1
1. C **3.** F **5.** D
2. E **4.** A **6.** B

Ex.2
1. B (to score an own goal)
2. D (to get the equaliser)
3. A (to concede a goal)
4. C (to take a deflection)

Ex.3
1. D (score with your left foot)
2. B (on 32 minutes)
3. F (winner for the home side)
4. E (in the 89th minute)
5. H (score against Rovers)
6. I (fifth goal of the season)
7. G (to go in front)
8. C (to come from a free kick)
9. A (to go behind = to concede a goal so now you have fewer goals than the other team)

Ex.4
1. E **2.** D **3.** A

4. C **5.** B

Ex.5

1. a)
2. b)
3. b)
4. b)
5. a) (to restore your lead = you led, then you lost the lead but now you lead again)
6. a)
7. b)
8. b)

Ex.6

1. an assist
2. composure
3. to finish
4. to set up (another player)
5. (score from) the rebound

Ex.7

1. G	**4.** F	**7.** A
2. E	**5.** C	**8.** D
3. B	**6.** H	

Ex.8

1. A	**4.** G	**7.** B
2. E	**5.** H	**8.** C
3. D	**6.** F	

10 SHOOTING

Ex.1

1. D 'hit it first time': to shoot with your first touch of the ball, without controlling the ball first.

2. A 'to hit the target': the shot is on the goal and will score a goal if the goalkeeper doesn't save it.

3. E 'to place it': to carefully and accurately shoot to a particular part of the goal, rather than shooting powerfully without much control over the exact direction of the shot.

4. C 'to shoot from a tight angle': to shoot from the side of the goal which means the shot has to be very accurate and it is relatively easy for the goalkeeper to save the shot.

5. B 'finishing': the skill of being calm, making the right decisions and shooting accurately when a player gets a chance to score.

Ex.2

1. (slotted) home
2. strike
3. fired (in)
4. back-lift
5. scuffed (his shot)

11 SKILLS & ABILITIES

Ex.1

1. B	**4.** F	**7.** H
2. G	**5.** C	**8.** E
3. A	**6.** D	

Ex.2

1. E/iii.
2. B/v.
3. A/iv.
4. C/i.
5. D/ii.

Ex.3

1. C/ii.
2. E/v.
3. D/i.
4. F/vi.
5. B/iii.
6. A/iv.

Ex.4

1. work-rate (how much physical effort a player makes)

2. shielding (protecting the ball with your body to stop an opponent getting it)

3. to have a burst of pace (to be able to run very fast over short distances)

4. holding up the ball (keeping possession of

the ball in an attacking position — without passing it — because there is no other player available to pass to yet)

5. to cover a lot of ground (to run a lot during a match)

6. a utility player (a player who is flexible and can play in various positions if the manager needs him to)

7. a box-to-box midfielder (a midfielder who is good at defending, attacking and scoring goals)

Ex.5

1. ii.   **3.** iii.   **5.** vi.
2. v.   **4.** iv.   **6.** i.

12 MANAGEMENT & SIGNINGS

Ex.1

1. team talk
2. transfer window
3. on (loan)
4. transfer fee
5. board (meeting)
6. appointed (this is a passive sentence: he **was** appoint**ed**)

Ex.2

1. transfer budget
2. (to) strengthen the

squad
3. a transfer target
4. wage demands
5. (to) sign (a player) on a free transfer
6. a contract extension
7. backroom staff (NB staff is an 'uncountable noun' — so ~~staffs~~ and ~~a staff~~ are incorrect)

Ex.3

1. Unveil: to formally announce that a new player or manager is joining a club. Often at a special event to which the media are invited.

2. To lose the dressing room: if a manager/coach has 'lost the dressing room' it means that the players no longer respect or listen to him. It is therefore very difficult for the manager to motivate the players and to make them play with his tactics. (The dressing room is the room in the stadium where the players change into their football kit before the game.)

3. Time to gel: if a team needs 'time to gel' it means that lots of the players are new, so they need time to learn about each other's playing style, and get used to the manager's tactics.

4. To be linked with: if a player or manager is 'linked with' another club, it means that there are rumours that he will move to that club.

5. A vote of confidence: a statement by the club to the media that they believe that their current manager is managing the team well. It happens when there is speculation in the media that a manager will be fired because of a team's poor form.

Ex.4

1. B/iv.
2. A/i.
3. C/v.
4. E/iii.
5. D/ii.

13 CHANCES

Ex.1

1. (a) great (effort!)
2. (a) fine (effort!)
3. (a) decent (effort!) [decent= "okay"]
4. (a) good (effort!)
5. (a) poor (effort!)

Ex.2

1. (an) easy (chance!)
2. (a) simple (chance!)

3. (a) decent/clear (chance!) [decent= "okay"]

4. (a) clear/decent (chance!)

5. (a) difficult (chance!)

6. (a) half (chance!)

Ex.3

1. to get a chance
2. to take a chance
3. to be unlucky
4. to create a chance
5. to find yourself free
6. to miss a chance

Ex.4

1. post
2. crossbar
3. save
4. tackle

Ex.5

1. C **4.** A **7.** E
2. G **5.** B
3. F **6.** D

Ex.6

1. to **squander a chance**/(opportunity) = to waste a chance; to miss a chance the player should have scored.

2. to **fluff a chance** = to miss a chance. The player is probably embarrassed because the chance was easy, or they made a big mistake.

3. **few and far between** = doesn't happen often.

4. **a chance goes begging** = a chance is missed, often a good chance.

5. **one on one** (with the keeper) = a situation where a player only has to get the ball past the goalkeeper to score a goal.

6. to **miss a sitter** = to miss a very, very easy chance

14 FORM

Ex.1

1. away form
2. in-form
3. inconsistent
4. result
5. performance

Ex.2

1. E (consistent)
2. D (4 in a row)
3. C (in their last 8)
4. A (performances)
5. F (results)
6. B (fine home form)

Ex.3

1. E **3.** D **5.** A
2. B **4.** C

Ex.4

1. C (unbeaten run of six games)
2. E (unbeaten in six games)
3. A (at home)
4. B (home record)
5. D (unbeaten in their last seven)
6. F (unbeaten in all competitions)

Ex.5

1. C (poor form)
2. E (decent form. Decent = 'okay')
3. B/A (fine/impressive)
4. A/B (impressive/fine)
5. D (top form)

15 STATISTICS

Ex.1

1. False (There were no red cards in the match).
2. True (Team B fouled Team A 10 times. Team A only fouled Team B 8 times).
3. False (**Possession**: the team has possession of the ball when their players are in control of the ball and passing it to each other).
4. True (**to book**: to give a player a yellow card).

5. True (**attempts on target**: shots and headers that will go in the goal if not stopped. **Attempts off target**: ones that will miss the goal. These add up to 14).

Ex.2

1. False (shots = 2).
2. True (an **assist**: when a player's pass or cross allows a teammate to score a goal).
3. False (**passing accuracy** %: the proportion of passes that successfully reach their target player).
4. False (**interception**: stopping another player's pass and taking the ball for yourself).
5. True (**key pass**: a pass which allows a teammate to shoot).

16 TEAM SELECTION

Ex.1

1. C **3.** A **5.** B
2. D **4.** E

Ex.2

1. B / rotate
2. D / (made the) bench
3. F / drop (him)
4. A / rotation (policy)
5. G / (pick a) full-strength (side)

6. C / (get his) place (back)
7. E / dropped

Ex.3

1. C/iii
2. A/iv
3. E/i
4. B/ii
5. F/v
6. D/vi

Ex.4

1. B/v
2. F/iv
3. E/i
4. C/ii
5. A/vi
6. D/iii

17 THE WORLD CUP

Ex.1

1. C/iv. "**World champions**: the winner of the World Cup is called this".
2. A/iii. "**Extra time**: the period of time over 90 minutes if a game ends with the scores level."
3. B/i. "**The group stages**: the part of the tournament where 4 teams play against each other in a 'mini-league'."

4. B/ii. "**The knockout stages**: the part of the tournament where the loser of a match has to leave the tournament."
5. D/v. "A **penalty shootout**: this is what happens if the scores are level after 120 minutes."
6. E/vi. "A **World Cup qualifier**: a match played before the World Cup to help decide which teams can go to the world cup."

Ex.2

1. The group stages
2. The second round
3. The quarter-finals
4. The semi-finals
5. The final

Ex.3

1. The first 'event' of the tournament = **opening ceremony**.
2. The group of players from which the team can be chosen = **squad**.
3. The official position in a list which rates how good international teams are = **FIFA ranking**.
4. To go through to the part of the tournament after the group stages = **to advance to the knockout stages**.

5. The team that finishes in first place in their 'mini-league' = **group winners**.

6. The team that finishes in *second* place in their 'mini-league' = **runners-up**.

7. The award given to the player who scores the most goals at the World Cup = **the Golden Boot**.

8. The 'song' which is played for each country before an international match = **national anthem**.

Ex.4

1. The event where the teams are put into their groups for the group stages: **the draw**.

2. A friendly match used as preparation: **warm up game**.

3. The number of times a player has played for their national team: **caps**.

4. The players and staff of a team at the World Cup: **the camp**.

5. The buildings, pitches and equipment etc. that a team uses to train: **training facilities**.

6. To attempt to become the hosts of a future World Cup: **to bid**.

7. To be given a special status which means that a highly ranked team won't have to play against other highly ranked teams at the group stages: **to be seeded**.

18   THE LEAGUE

Ex.1

1. G	**4.** D	**7.** F
2. B	**5.** A	**8.** C
3. E	**6.** H	

Ex.2

1. C (top of the league)

2. A (to win the league) (NB 'to win' is an irregular verb: *win, won*, have *won*.)

3. E (to get promotion)

4. F (bottom of the league)

5. B (to avoid relegation)

6. D (to go down)

Ex.3

1. got (to get promotion)

2. relegation (to avoid relegation)

3. get (to get into the play-off places)

4. -offs (the play-offs)

5. finished (to finish in the play-off places)

6. places (the relegation places)

7. goal (goal difference: the number of goals a team scores *minus* the number of goals a team concedes. NB the preposition which goes with this word in 'on', e.g. 'We are level **on** goal difference)

Ex.4

1. true

2. true

3. false (but, for instance, Hillford & Sommerhill are level on points)

4. true

5. false

6. true

7. true

8. true

9. true (there are normally 4 play-off places in the English divisions)

10. false (3 teams are normally relegated in the English divisions)

11. true

12. false (they are 4 points behind)

13. true

14. true

15. false

16. false

17. true (they have the same number of points as Bridgeforth but a better goal difference)

18. true

19. false (they are 8 points clear of the relegation zone)

20. true (two more points would mean they would be out of the relegation zone)

21. false

22. true

Ex.5

1. the run in
2. stay top
3. drop points at home
4. mid-table
5. closed the gap
6. have moved up three places
7. the drop zone
8. a game in hand

19 FOOTBALL GROUNDS & THE PITCH

Ex.1

1. video screen
2. stand
3. turnstile
4. executive boxes
5. coach
6. stewards

Ex.2

1. E
2. L [Officially the goal line is the whole line, from corner to corner, but people normally use it to mean the line between the goal posts only.]
3. C
4. K
5. I
6. G
7. A
8. F
9. H
10. B
11. J
12. D

Ex.3

1. dressing room
2. capacity
3. tier
4. tunnel
5. attendance
6. end

20 MISTAKES

Ex.1

1. C	3. C	5. A
2. E	4. B	6. D

Ex.2

1. a misplaced pass
2. (to be) caught in possession / (to be) dispossessed
3. to switch off / a lapse of concentration

Ex.3

1. (To) **blast over**: to shoot at goal very powerfully and miss because the ball goes much too high over the goal.

2. A **defensive blunder**: a very bad mistake made when defending (which often leads to the other team scoring a goal).

3. (To drop) **a clanger**: to make a very bad mistake (which often leads to the other team scoring a goal).

4. (To be) **undone** (by): to be beaten/defeated (or to concede an equaliser which means you draw a game you really should have won).

21 TRAINING

Ex.1

1. F	3. E	5. D
2. C	4. A	6. B

Ex.2

1. a session
2. sprints
3. a drill

4. a five-a-side
5. stretches

Ex.3

1. G; passing and moving
2. C; creating/making space
3. E; ball control
4. A; accurate passing
5. D; set pieces
6. F; retaining possession
7. B; making yourself available

Ex.4

1. C; two-touch
2. H; cool down
3. A; keep-ups
4. D; chalkboard
5. G; awareness
6. E; body shape
7. F; plant foot
8. B; movement

22   CALLS

Ex.1

1. D
2. B
3. F
4. G
5. E
6. H
7. K
8. C
9. L

10. I [opposite = "Near post!"]
11. J
12. A

23   INJURIES

Ex.1

1. B   **4.** D   **7.** F
2. G   **5.** C   **8.** H
3. A   **6.** E

Ex.2

1. iv/A
2. i/D
3. vi/E
4. iii/B
5. ii/A
6. vii/C
7. v/F

Ex.3

1. to be stretchered off
2. a collision
3. to be sidelined
4. to pick up a knock
5. an injury crisis
6. (to be) on the treatment table
7. prognosis
8. (to be) hamstrung
9. to suffer a setback

24   FANS

Ex.1

1. B
2. C
3. B (NB the fans **aren't** very loud...)
4. A
5. D

Ex.2

1. B
2. E
3. A
4. F
5. C
6. D

Ex.3

1. A **season ticket**: a small book containing tickets for home matches for one year.
2. (To give someone/ something a) **muted reception**: to welcome someone or something *less* enthusiastically than normal.
3. (To) **buoy** (someone): to make someone feel confident and hopeful.
4. (To) **boo**: to make a noise which shows you do *not* like something.

5. A **pitch invasion**: when hundreds of fans run on to the playing area during or after a match.

6. (A) **cheer**: a noise which shows you *do* like something. (Can also be used as a verb: 'to cheer'.)

25   THE GOAL

Ex.1

1. A   **3.** D   **5.** E
2. F   **4.** B   **6.** C

Ex.2

1. post
2. off
3. over
4. rattled (the shot was very hard and made the crossbar vibrate)
5. woodwork

Ex.3

1. 'over the bar'
2. 'to rattle the crossbar'
3. 'to be saved by the woodwork'
4. 'to strike the post' / 'to come off the post'

26   FIXTURES

Ex.1

1. fixture list

2. derbies (singular = a derby)
3. the opening day (of the season)
4. (the) run in
5. campaign

Ex.2

1. F/ii (a cup tie)
2. A/v (an early kick-off)
3. D/iii (the ticket allocation)
4. E/iv (the second leg)
5. B/i (a midweek game)
6. C/vi (the close season)

Ex.3

1. D   **3.** C
2. B   **4.** A

27   GOALKEEPING

Ex.1

1. The keeper made a great save.
2. That was a fine save from the keeper.
3. The keeper saved with his feet.
4. The keeper punched the ball away from danger.
5. The defender left it for the keeper.

Ex.2

1. F   **4.** C   **7.** G
2. A   **5.** E
3. D   **6.** B

Ex.3

1. F/ii.
2. A/iii.
3. E/i.
4. C/vi.
5. B/v.
6. D/iv.

Ex.4

1. C/iii.
2. E/ii.
3. D/v.
4. A/i.
5. B/iv.

28   HEADING

Ex.1

1. B   **3.** E   **5.** C
2. A   **4.** D

Ex.2

1. C   **3.** A   **5.** B
2. D   **4.** E

29   TIMING

Ex.1

1. E   **3.** A   **5.** C
2. B   **4.** D

Ex.2

1. D **3.** E **5.** A
2. C **4.** B

30 MISCELLANEOUS

Ex.1

1. B (**highlights**: the best parts of a match).
2. F (**world class player**: a player who is one of the best in his position in the whole world).
3. E (**replay**: the 'extra' match which is played if the game finishes in a draw in a cup competition).
4. A (**captain's armband**: the band around a player's arm which shows he is the captain).
5. C (**kit**: the clothes that players wear in matches).
6. D (**a yard**: 0.91 metres)

Ex.2

1. Different. A television commentator describes a match as it happens. A television presenter is responsible for presenting the television programme, for instance leading the discussion at half-time.
2. The same. In the United Kingdom; soccer is a synonym for football. Different in the United States; football normally means 'American Football'.
3. Different. The underdogs are the team which most people think will lose a match.
4. The same, e.g. "On Saturday it's United against/versus City."
5. Different. The Football Association is the organisation responsible for all football in a country. The Premier League is the organisation responsible for the top league in England.
6. The same. The 'cups' etc. which the captain of the team is presented with when they win a league or a cup competition. (NB you can say 'a trophy', but you can't say "a silverware' - it is an uncountable noun.)

Ex.3

1. E (in the air)
2. C (on the ground)
3. D (to put ten men behind the ball)
4. A (to go down to ten men)
5. G (to put out a strong team)

6. F (to be tied against [a team in a cup competition]. If team A are tied against team B, it means they will play against each other)
7. B (to retire from the game)

Ex.4

1. E/iii (an outside chance)
2. D/ii (away strip)
3. B/v (to be cup tied)
4. A/i (winning mentality)
5. C/iv (shin pads)

Ex.5

1. C/iii (a loose ball)
2. D/vi (to be a lot at stake)
3. E/v (match fixing)
4. F/ii (gamesmanship)
5. B/i (grassroots football)
6. A/iv (a journeyman)

Printed in Great Britain
by Amazon